Using Theory in Youth and Community Work Practice

Titles in the Series

To order, please contact our distributor: BEBC Distribution, Albion Close, Parkstone, Poole, BH12 3LL. Telephone: 0845 230 9000, email: learningmatters@bebc.co.uk.

You can also find more information on each of these titles and our other learning resources at www.learningmatters.co.uk.

Using Theory in Youth and Community Work Practice

EDITED BY ILONA BUCHROTH AND CHRIS PARKIN

Series Editors: Janet Batsleer and Keith Popple

First published in 2010 by Learning Matters Ltd

British Library Cataloguing in Publication Data
A CIP record for this book is available from the British Library.

ISBN 978 1 84445 300 9

Cover and text design by Code 5 Design Associates Ltd
Project management by Swales & Willis Ltd, Exeter, Devon
Typeset by Swales & Willis Ltd, Exeter, Devon
Printed and bound in Great Britain by TJ International Ltd, Padstow, Cornwall

Learning Matters Ltd
33 Southernhay East
Exeter EX1 1NX
Tel: 01392 215560
info@learningmatters.co.uk
www.learningmatters.co.uk

FSC
Mixed Sources
Product group from well-managed
forests and other controlled sources
Cert no. SGS-COC-2482
www.fsc.org
© 1996 Forest Stewardship Council

Contents

We would like to dedicate this book to our inspiring students
and fieldwork colleagues

Foreword from the Series Editors

Youth work and community work has a long, rich and diverse history that spans three centuries. The development of youth work extends from the late nineteenth and early twentieth century with the emergence of voluntary groups and the serried ranks of the UK's many uniformed youth organisations, through to modern youth club work, youth project work, and informal education. Youth work remains, in the early twenty-first century, a mixture of voluntary effort and paid and state sponsored activity.

Community work also had its beginnings in voluntary activity. Some of this activity was in the form of 'rescuing the poor', while community action developed as a response to oppressive circumstances and was based on the idea of self-help. In the second half of the twentieth century the state financed a good deal of local authority and government sponsored community and regeneration work and now there are multi-various community action projects and campaigns.

Today there are thousands of people involved in youth work and community work both in paid positions and in voluntary roles. However, the activity is undergoing significant change. National Occupation Standards and a new academic benchmarking statement have recently been introduced, and soon all youth and community workers undertaking qualifying courses and who successfully graduate will do so with an honours degree.

Empowering Youth and Community Work Practice is a series of texts primarily aimed at students on youth and community work courses. However, more experienced practitioners from a wide range of fields will find these books useful because they offer effective ways of integrating theory, knowledge and practice. Written by experienced lecturers, practitioners, and policy commentators each title covers core aspects of what is needed to be an effective practitioner and will address key competences for professional JNC recognition as a youth and community worker. The books use case studies, activities, and references to the latest government initiatives to help readers learn and develop their theoretical understanding and practice. This series will provide invaluable support to anyone studying or practicing in the field of youth and community work as well as a number of other related fields.

Janet Batsleer
Manchester Metropolitan University

Keith Popple
London South Bank University

Introduction

This book has been written for undergraduate students of community and youth work and will be of equal relevance to other related professions working at a community level. The book's main emphasis is on exploring various theoretical perspectives that underlie the range of practice tasks involved in these professions.

From our experience of teaching community and youth work it appears that the relationship between theory and practice is not always an easy one for our students. Many students and practitioners approach theory sceptically and at times reluctantly and tend to view the pursuit of theory and practice as separate concerns. This separation between theorists and practitioners is worth exploring in its own right because, as we will argue throughout this book, it reflects a particular distribution of power in the way different views and perspectives are heard and valued.

Overview

Chapter 1 explores theory as a concept and links it to the role it plays in professional work. It looks at how theory is developed and how issues of power and equality relate to the way we use, choose and take part in the development of theory. This chapter encourages readers to use their curiosity and practical knowledge to find answers and explanations for the situations that community and youth workers encounter in their practice.

Chapter 2 has a focus on social theory and its relevance to community and youth work practice. It will introduce readers to a range of different social theories before considering the way in which theory explains communities and the way in which power operates in society.

Chapter 3 looks at life experiences and how theory can be used to explore how values and beliefs are developed. It is concerned with the way people look at their lives, tell their stories and make sense of them within a wider social and political context. It helps readers to understand how their own identity can assist them in understanding the lives of young people and adults they work with.

Chapter 4 looks at education in the wider sense. It explores some of the underlying concepts that make up and shape educational experiences, how learning is influenced by a range of different forces within society, and how these interact with and are shaped by power. These theoretical considerations invite professional workers to critically examine the educational aspects of their role.

Chapter 5 asserts the centrality of group work in community and youth work with particular reference to fostering democratic working and seeking collective solutions to identified issues. It explores groups from a wide variety of angles and covers concepts and methods which reflect upon the equality and power issues associated with empowerment practices in the areas of inclusion, group communication, roles, leadership and evaluative tasks.

Chapter 6 explores the nature of reflection and its place in professional practice. It covers some of the main theoretical perspectives and looks at a sample of the tools that can be employed to help with reflective processes. This chapter focuses on the role of supervision and in particular solution-focused supervision using the Appreciative enquiry model as it provides an empowering framework for workers in their practice.

Learning features

This book is designed to enable you to take an active part in reading it. There is a wide range of activities and case studies in each chapter which will help you to understand theory and more importantly relate it to your practice. This book is not designed to be read from cover to cover in one go. We expect that you will dip in and out depending on the particular aspect of theory you are interested in; however, we would urge you to read Chapter 1 first as this chapter introduces you to the concept and use of theory. You will also find that there are links between the chapters so that for example in selecting Chapter 4 your attention will be drawn to relevant sections of Chapters 2 and 3.

National Occupational Standards and Subject Benchmarks

The National Occupational Standards in Youth Work were published early in 2008 and represent the latest agreed 'range of functions undertaken across youth work, across the public and voluntary sectors' (LLUK, 2008). The full set of standards is available from the Lifelong Learning Website (**www.lluk.org.uk**; see Figure 1.1). This book is concerned with the underpinning knowledge required to carry out these functions and relates to all five functions, though the emphasis is on the knowledge required to plan and carry out face-to-face work with young people (Functions 1–4):

- facilitate the personal, social and educational development of young people;
- promote equality and young people's interests and welfare;
- work with others;
- develop youth work strategy and practice.

At the beginning of each chapter we have specified which occupational standards will be supported by the theoretical perspectives outlined in the chapter and in most cases we have referred to the first level functions and specified the areas of knowledge which support these functions.

Subject benchmarks for youth and community work are published on the Quality Assurance Agency for Higher Education (QAA) Website **www.qaa.ac.uk** – these benchmarks are particularly helpful in indicating the subject knowledge and understanding required to support the functions of youth and community work.

The benchmark statement identifies four broad areas of subject knowledge:

1   working in and with communities;

2   working with young people; working with adults;

3   approaches to learning and development;

4   developing community-based organisations.

The statement stresses that all areas of learning are interconnected and that the aim of study is to develop critical reflective practitioners. The understanding and use of theory is in our view central to critical reflective practice. The chapters in this book focus on the underpinning theory which supports these areas of knowledge. The benchmark statement identifies a set of benchmark standards which represent the knowledge, skills and understanding that students should be able to evidence on completion of an undergraduate programme of study in youth and community work. At the beginning of each chapter we have identified the standards that will be supported by the content of the chapter.

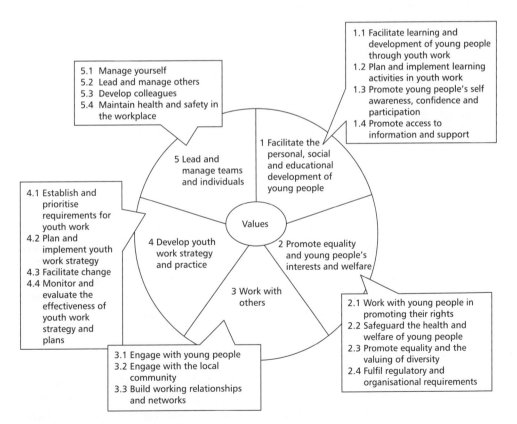

Figure 1.1 National Occupational Standards for Youth Work. Source: LLUK (2008)

Chapter 1
Theory and Youth and Community Work Practice

Ilona Buchroth and Chris Parkin

CHAPTER OBJECTIVES

This chapter is about the use of theory in relation to practice and consequently it will help you to address all areas of the National Occupational Standards for Youth Work. In particular the creative approach to developing and using theory developed in the chapter will help you to address the following Standards.

1.1.3 Encourage young people to broaden their horizons to be active citizens

2.3.2 Develop a culture and systems that promote equality and value diversity

4.2.1 Influence and support the development of youth work strategies

It will also introduce you to the following academic standards as set out in the youth and community work benchmark statement (2009, QAA).

7.1
- Recognise and compare multiple, competing perspectives and challenge the status quo and dominant perspectives.
- Question and be prepared to deconstruct taken for granted and common sense professional understandings.

Introduction

This chapter is concerned with what theory is and its relevance to practice; it is about the theory of developing and applying theory. More specifically it explores the role theory plays in professional work and aims to identify the different kinds of theory we come across and make use of. A second strand of the chapter looks at how theory is developed and how it is linked to our professional roles. Finally, we explore how issues of power and equality relate to the way we use, choose and take part in the development of theory.

What do we actually mean when we talk about theory?

Dictionary entries vary, but all will suggest some form of statement that refers to an organised framework or model that helps us understand particular phenomena. It is useful to explain what theory is by distinguishing between facts, concepts and theory. Facts are verifiable assertions about some specific element of the world – for example, there are 45 students in my class, the grass is green, the house is made of bricks, 30 per cent of households in my city are headed by a single parent. Sometimes even facts are disputed – for example, what is green? How do you know that the colour I see as green is the same as the colour you see? Sometimes we will dispute whether the facts are indeed facts – for example, how was the information collected in determining that 30 per cent of households were headed by a single parent? Is 30 per cent an estimate based on a small sample? Is it possible that the figures are inaccurate because in reality people work to different definitions of 'single parent'?

In social life there are few facts; we tend to deal with concepts such as the family, education, adolescence, deviance, equality. Concepts are something conceived in our minds and are abstract or generalised ideas. We have an idea about what concepts are but our ideas will vary. For example, let us look at family. I might think of my family as my partner and child; others might include parents, grandparents and siblings; some of you may include friends. In some cultures family may include all members of a tribe or clan. In order to explain concepts we develop theory – a systematic way of explaining concepts. The term 'theory' is used quite loosely in general conversation to describe ideas or 'hunches' people might have about how things can be done or explained. However, for something to be described as a theory it needs to go beyond a simple idea; it needs to be based on evidence and be testable in the broadest sense. The process of developing theory is often based on research and this will be explored later in the chapter. As we will also see later, theories developed within the natural sciences or within a positivist framework usually have a more tightly defined approach to what might be accepted as evidence or what form of scrutiny a theory needs to be able to withstand. For the purpose of this chapter we will adopt a similar approach to the one outlined by Henry Mintzberg (2005) who, rather than wishing to give a precise definition of the term 'theory', first asserts his keen interest in finding explanations. The process of finding explanations, he suggests, develops along a continuum that starts with making lists and categories, through establishing relationships and patterns to seeking explanations for patterns and relationships. In a similar vein this chapter has been written within a mindset that values curiosity and imagination – to create theories about all manner of things, to find a range of different explanations for the situations we encounter, to be alert and keen to ask imaginative questions, rather than knowing the answers as *theory is insightful when it surprises, when it allows us to see profoundly, imaginatively, unconventionally into phenomena that we thought we understood* (Mintzberg, 2005, p361).

An introduction to using theory

Starting with theory and the role it plays in our lives we soon realise that we engage with a range of different perspectives on numerous occasions. Try to answer the question in Activity 1.1.

ACTIVITY 1.1

In your everyday life do you make use of theory?

Examples might include how to bring up children to become happy and fulfilled adults, how best to stop global warming, or how to deal with stress. Can you think of any more examples and can you identify what theory you are using?

In all of the examples above you are likely to consciously or subconsciously use and apply theory. Your theory about child rearing is likely to draw on a whole range of other theories – for example, psychological theories such as child development, learning theories, social theories to explore the role of the family, education, culture and media as well as scientific theory to consider the role of nutrition, exercise and the impact of environmental factors such as pollution.

If you are talking to others you will find that not everyone agrees with your take on theory and they might well want to emphasise a different approach. Your parents or grandparents will have used different theories to guide them through their parenting and their ideas about what constitutes a healthy diet are likely to be quite different from yours too. What does this tell us about theory?

- It reminds us that theories are not fixed, but that they develop and change over time usually as a result of research and reflection on experience.

- It shows us that theory can be 'fashionable'; certain approaches and viewpoints come and go and depend on what the dominant current issues or perspectives are. For example, many recent government policies related to overcoming disadvantage are influenced by the concept of social capital (also see Chapters 2 and 4).

- Certain theory can be promoted to meet particular ends.

- Theory is not good, bad, true or false, but often just more useful for one application or another (Mintzberg, 2005, p356).

Activity 1.2 reflects on this in relation to theories about drug addiction.

ACTIVITY **1.2**

Try to answer these questions drawing on any experience or knowledge you have.

- *What are drugs?*

- *What is addiction?*

- *What causes drug addiction?*

- *How can drug addiction be treated?*

Theories about what constitutes a drug and what counts as addiction have changed over time. In the nineteenth century the use of opium was not illegal and was widely used as an over-the-counter remedy for a range of ailments. It is only relatively recently that cigarettes have been considered as a drug or an addiction.

There is a range of theories linked to the cause of addiction, including:

- personality trait – genetically disposed to addictions;

- poverty – drugs offer escape from harsh reality of life;

- economic – drug suppliers need to make drugs acceptable to increase profit or individuals use drugs to improve performance in order to earn more money;

- deviance – drugs are linked to criminal behaviour.

You may have identified others. There is also a range of theories linked to how to treat addictions:

- harm reduction;

- treatment with substitutes, e.g. nicotine patches, methadone;

- complete withdrawal;

- prevention.

In looking at this range we can see that different theories have been more dominant or fashionable in dealing with addictions. In particular the harm reduction approach is currently popular. We can also see that pharmaceutical companies might promote the use of drug substitutes rather than complete withdrawal, as this will generate profits for them. Similarly, some health workers may favour harm reduction because they gain employment if this approach is used. Finally, the theories about the causes of drug addiction and indeed the treatment may all be 'right' in certain circumstances.

Theory in relation to Community and Youth Work

We want to suggest that there is not one body of theory of community and youth work but many different and sometimes contradictory theories. There is a range of theories about:

- *why* we do community and youth work;

- *how* we do community and youth work;

- *what* community and youth work encompasses.

These are usually hard questions to answer and we need to use some kind of theory to come up with those answers. Try asking your colleagues what they think about these questions. You could try asking other people the answers to these questions and get a wide range of different answers. You might want to discount some answers because you think the person you ask doesn't know anything about youth work; you may discount others because you don't think they are very good youth workers; you may agree partly with some answers but have a slightly different perspective. If you had to write an essay responding to these questions it is likely that you would refer to published articles, reports or books addressing these questions. For example, you might look at the National Youth Agency's publications – books such as *The Art of Youth Work* by Kerry Young or *The History of Youth Work* by Bernard Davies. Or you could look at journals such as *Children and Young People Now* and *Youth and Policy* as well as Websites such as **www.infed.org/**. It is likely that you would also use your own experiences – maybe drawing on your own participation in youth work as a young person as well as your current employment. However, you are also likely to draw on your beliefs about what young people need; these beliefs are often the result of a range of factors, as you will see from Chapter 3. The answers to these questions are the substance of what theory is and you should be able to see that theory is central to your practice because it helps you and others to explain why you do the work, how you do it and the results of your work. There is now a wealth of theory on youth work – much of this relates to the history, purpose and process of the work. This book will guide you through theories which underpin youth work rather than provide a review of these theories.

Not using theory in a professional role must be akin to needing to re-invent the wheel and starting afresh every single day. Some practitioners suggest that theory is of secondary importance in youth work practice and that the most important thing is the ability to listen to young people and provide them with space. While we would not wish to dispute that listening to young people is important, we agree with Spence that:

> *Listening effectively and actively requires some knowledge on the part of the worker. They might need to know something of youth subcultures, but under this, they might need to know something about class and poverty, about racism and sexism, about the realities of global displacement, about structural relations of power in which some voices are silenced and in which listening must be an active process of encouraging speaking, not just the speaking of individuals, though that is important, but the speaking which enables groups to find collective voices and thus to combine and act on their situation.* (Spence, 'In Defence of Youth Work' Leeds, 10 July 2009)

Although we might not always use theory consciously our understanding of a range of relationships and patterns guides us in numerous ways. We may have been in similar situations before and we apply an understanding of different situations to a new setting. We have some understanding of the issues that are important in the lives of the people we work with. So we have established that we can use theory to help us to think about the purpose and process of our practice but it is important to remember that we can also develop theory *from* our practice. Our experience of practice provides us with evidence to challenge or support theoretical perspectives.

We will have observed others' practice, read reports of practice and talked to young people about their lives, and we draw on all of these things to develop effective work. In an informal way we also use these experiences to develop our own theory. We hope that this chapter will encourage you to be more conscious of the way in which you use theory, and encourage you to develop and test your theories in relation to the theories that have been written up and tested by people who you may think of as theorists or academics.

We have been trying to emphasise in this section that the 'usefulness' of theory depends very much on your standpoint and perspective. As a result the theoretical perspectives that we highlight in this book start with the central ingredient of community and youth work – that is, a critical appraisal of power relationships and the resulting social justice issues that arise out of these for our work. So in our definition of usefulness we have been concentrating on the theoretical underpinnings that help us both understand how power relationships work and how we can be most effective in our professional roles. You might also define usefulness in terms of your values and beliefs and therefore discount theories that are in conflict with them.

Types of theory and their use in practice

Formal and informal theory

This book is primarily concerned with the relationship between formal theories – those which have been tested and have legitimacy among specialists in the subject, and how they shape and explain community and youth work. However, our understanding of the world and therefore our practice is also quite significantly influenced by what can be termed 'informal' knowledge and theory. Juliette Oko (2008), writing about theory in social work, distinguishes between the kind of informal theory that is formed by our 'common sense' and taken for granted ideas about life in general and those that are transmitted within a practice context. Both of these sources imply some form of 'practical wisdom', the origins of which might well be rooted in established practice and are often quite difficult to trace. For example, our judgement of what we think is happening and why is quite likely to be influenced by the way we were brought up, what our values are, what we consider to be 'normal' or acceptable. Similarly, we will learn ways of working from experienced practitioners and our appreciation of practice issues and approaches to the work will be shaped by their practical wisdom. We would urge caution in relying on this 'common sense' approach to theory because one person's common sense can be another's nonsense. However, it is still useful to draw on these experiences and engage in critical reflection which will enable us to 'test' our informal theories.

Espoused theory and theory in use

Smith (1994), drawing on Argyris and Schön, suggests distinguishing between what he refers to as 'espoused' theory and 'theory-in-use'. If, for example, we were having a conversation about an approach to a hypothetical situation, your answer would be quite likely to contain your 'espoused' theory – you would talk about an ideal response. However, your actual behaviour might reveal a different approach: not one that is devoid of theory, but one that makes use of a different theory. For example, if you were outlining to somebody else how you think it is best to engage young people you might say that you work with young people in an empowering way by being non-judgemental, being interested in their lives and approachable. In reality, colleagues or young people may observe that this is not always the case – either because you fall short of your own expressed expectations (e.g. you are often so busy doing paperwork that you refuse to talk to a young person or may even be dismissive of the young people) or that you actually generally work to a different theory from the one you outlined (e.g. you generally plan lots of exciting activities and rely on your charisma and energy to carry people along).

As a reflective practitioner it is therefore not only important to be mindful of the various influences on our practice and to remain open to seeking different explanations, but also to examine the relationship between our theories in use and those we claim to adhere to. Especially as an experienced worker you will carry out many tasks in an almost intuitive manner and of course that intuition makes a valuable contribution to the richness of your action and judgement. Indeed, it would almost be impossible to work without making use of routines or sometimes going with your 'gut-feeling'. However, experience and intuition can be restricting forces as well, and both 'reflection in action' and 'on action' are the essentials of improving practice. (We will look at this in more detail in Chapter 6.)

Conflicting theories

As we have seen earlier, theories evolve over time and are promoted for a range of different reasons; they are not true or false, but they can serve different purposes. It is therefore also likely that we will find that theories contradict each other or seem to suggest widely different approaches. Critical reflection requires us not to take polarised views, but to carefully dismantle theoretical perspectives for their respective merit. It is here that we would like to emphasise the importance of asking questions rather than the need to find answers.

ACTIVITY 1.3

Think of some of your firmly held views on your practice – for example, your views on barring young people from youth clubs for 'unacceptable' behaviour.

- *When and why is it necessary to bar young people?*

- *When and why shouldn't young people be barred?*

- *What are the limitations of each position – that is, even if you think barring is not a good idea, are there occasions when you would consider it?*

- *What are the consequences of barring or not barring young people?*

- *What is the premise on which you make these decisions?*

- *What would 'acceptable' behaviour constitute in this context?*

- *How do your organisation's policies impact on decisions to bar young people?*

Activity 1.3 is likely to have brought out a good range of different perspectives. In particular it aimed to highlight that there might be different approaches to different situations and that often it is not useful to take an absolute position without careful consideration of its appropriateness for any given situation. A critical testing of theoretical perspectives can then lead to refinements and modifications, and new theories are created.

In addition to testing theories for their relevance, as practitioners we are also likely to find ourselves in positions where we have to deal with conflicting theories. The conflict may arise from our own value base and views on 'what is right' or we could find ourselves faced with a dilemma. A dilemma is usually a position that has two approaches we agree with, but applying one will cancel out the other. Sometimes these dilemmas are more explicitly linked to theory – for example, in considering issues of power. If we acknowledge that there is a network of practices and institutions in society which effectively control people and consequently do not need to assert their power in an explicit way, then we might argue that groups who are disempowered as a result of this need to be engaged in a conscience-raising group in order to begin to recognise the way in which they are oppressed. This theory is frequently used to support girls' work in single gender groups. However, we might also argue that the best way to change the way in which groups are disempowered requires 'emancipatory' learning, whereby groups come together to learn to work co-operatively. This would suggest that it would be best to work in mixed groups so that groups can share their common understanding of oppressive systems. This leaves us with a dilemma: should we work in single sex groups or mixed groups?

In dealing with a dilemma we are reminded that we are not often in a position where we can find a 'correct' answer to a problem. As a result we are not just applying theory in a mechanical way; we are required to engage with theory in quite an in-depth way that will help us to exercise professional judgement. Mark Smith suggests that in order to make these professional judgements we need to be guided by our general disposition and values that help us seek a 'good' and 'right' decision – one that *makes for human well being* and helps us to *act truly and justly* (Smith, 1994, p76). In our earlier example a 'good' decision therefore would be one that we feel would serve the people involved best under the given circumstances.

This approach does not always work without difficulties or without creating further dilemmas. As we will discuss in more detail in Chapter 4, room for making professional judgements can be constrained and meeting the demands of different lines of accountability can further limit the opportunities to depart from preset agendas.

Another instance of conflicting theory arises from the possibility that people we work with may perform within different theoretical frameworks. Increasingly, as we work in integrated settings, other professionals working to different priorities and agendas will also have different sets of values and perspectives. Here we need to be reminded again that no theory is 'true', but more a representation of reality from a particular, chosen angle. This idea is explored more in Chapter 2 in relation to a range of perspectives that will result in different priorities for practice. For example, referring to theories of social capital, those working with Putnam's theories are likely to focus on increasing the numbers of people engaged with community and voluntary groups, whereas those working with Bourdieu's theories are likely to work towards challenging the power relationships, thereby focusing on the way in which participation in voluntary groups helps people to recognise and challenge their oppression. Rather than viewing theories as being in competition with each other, our professional judgement may well be enhanced by our truly engaging with another viewpoint. *Knowledge is not a fixed thing or a commodity to be grasped . . . it is rather an aspect of a process* (Smith, 1994, p157). The aim therefore is not to win or lose an argument, but to move beyond our own 'horizon of understanding' and widen it to accommodate another perspective. This is particularly important when we think about our commitment to developing work with people that starts with their concerns. What is required here is to listen carefully to how people actually make sense of their lives rather than overlaying their views with our interpretation of reality. This can make for some delicate engagement with theory that both sides can learn and develop from.

ACTIVITY **1.4**

A young community and youth worker was involved in a project aimed at reducing unemployment among young people. Her theory on how to increase employment chances, supported by some statistical evidence but most importantly borne out by her own life experience, was centred on increasing educational attainment. The link was so firmly embedded in her thinking that she immediately embarked on organising a series of educational courses. She made a real effort to find out what the local skill shortages were, talked to local businesses and consulted with young people about what they wanted to learn, where and when to hold classes and groups.

What do you think happened?

Unfortunately it was not the success it was hoped it would be and hardly anybody came along. By talking to people in different circumstances it became clearer that many people worked to different 'theories' – for example, the best way to get a job is 'to be in the right place at the right time'. Although some young people saw the link between education and work they did not think it applied to them. This example showed two things: that the worker's consultation did not include questioning her own basic premise; and that, because the dominant discourse also supports the link between education and employment, the young people were unlikely to have challenged the worker.

Linking theory to practice

In this section we will explore ways in which theory is used in practice. We will consider ways in which we choose which theory to draw on and how we can develop theory from practice. We begin with a case study.

CASE STUDY

Anti-social behaviour?

You are a community worker in a local area and are being told that there is now a group of young people hanging around a public area near the local shops. One of the shopkeepers is not too happy and tells you that their customers are being intimidated by the young people's presence and this might affect business.

What is your first response to this scenario? What do you think is happening there? Do you have sympathy with the shopkeeper, the local people or the young people? What is your explanation for the scenario? What do you think is the background to the situation?

We want to use this case study to look at aspects of relating theory to practice. First, we will consider how to use and choose theory to help us understand the scenario and how we should respond. Second, we will explore how your efforts in understanding and responding to this situation can help you to develop theory.

Your interpretation of the situation is likely to be guided by your existing knowledge and understanding of the local area as well as what you know about young people's interests and behaviour. Rather than looking at the scenario afresh, you will interpret it in the light of your existing knowledge – you will link it to an underlying theoretical perspective.

The link to theory can be undertaken in essentially two different ways: it can be a process of *deduction* or *induction*.

- Deduction is broadly concerned with testing theory – we are looking at how general concepts are realised in the particular instances that we are working within.

- Induction refers to this process in reverse – it looks at particular, specific data and tries to generalise from it – it refers to the creation of theory.

These two processes are interdependent and theory development is therefore often a cyclical process where new theories are developed from new data and then tested again in practice and revised as a result.

Let us see how deduction and induction can be applied to our scenario above. What was your 'hunch' when you first heard the story? Maybe you were not altogether surprised that young people gathering in public spaces elicits a negative response. From your own experience in other situations and as an avid reader of relevant professional journals you will of course be aware that it is very common to portray young people as a threat as soon as they are seen meeting as a group. In this case you would see the comments of the shopkeeper and the public as confirmation of a theory that refers to the negative public image of young people.

However, you might actually look into the issues in more depth and reveal a whole range of factors that you had not been aware of, or be encouraged to link factors in ways that they had not been linked before. This could put you into a good position to look at the information afresh and see whether you can generalise from this particular scenario and if the conclusions that you draw could be applied to other settings. This means you are using your information in an inductive way and hence you can be involved in the creation of theory.

Returning to Mintzberg's take on theory earlier, he suggests that all *theories are false. They are, after all, just words and symbols . . . about the reality they purport to describe; they are not that reality. . . .This means we must choose our theories according to how useful they are, not how true they are* (Mintzberg, 2005, p356).

What does useful theory mean for us in this context? If we return to the issues outlined in the case study, we could now look at a whole range of theoretical perspectives to help us both understand what is happening and what might be the best way to intervene. There will be theories which help to explain *why* the young people are gathering. For example, we could explore a psychological dimension to explain why people need to gather in groups and why and how collective behaviour differs from individual behaviour. Alternatively we could draw on social theory and explain their behaviour as either an indicator that structures in society such as schools and families are not working properly or even that the behaviour of the young people is a legitimate/normal response to the oppression that young people experience.

There will be theories which help us to think about *how* to approach the young people: this may include a public order approach looking at the way crowds are dispersed and the sanctions that can be put in place to stop the group gathering again. But are any of these theories 'useful' to you as a community and youth worker? There are surely occasions when any of these could be of relevance, but the question you need to ask yourself here is *what* do you want to achieve as a community and youth worker overall? Your answers might vary and are likely to include some or all of the following.

- Promote and improve the rights of young people – you may want to challenge the notion that groups of young people are problematic. *This approach could be informed by your understanding of inequality and could be linked to social theory.*

- Support the young people in gaining access to activities which will help them to realise their potential and make a positive contribution to society by exploring ways of engaging young people in pursuits that are meaningful to them. *This approach is likely to be informed by your experience of working with young people or your own experiences as a young person. The approach could be informed by your understanding of informal education.*

- Support the young people to make choices for themselves. *This approach is also likely to be informed by your own experiences but could also be informed by your understanding of theories linked to empowerment or group work.*

- Support the young people to secure suitable places to gather and associate with each other in informal ways. *This approach could be linked to your understanding of the purpose of youth work and supported by your understanding of collective action.*

We have outlined some theoretical perspectives which might be 'useful' to you. These may help you decide on a specific approach to the problem but you will also need to draw on theory that will help you in actually carrying out your practice. What kinds of knowledge and insights have you got already? Where would you look for further ideas and explanations? Our guess is that your search might take you to see what detached youth workers have got to say on how best to make contact with young people on their own territory. Maybe some ideas about group work might come in handy. Equally, writers on informal education could help your thinking on methods of learning linked to empowerment. You might explore ideas about organising around shared and common issues. In reflecting on your existing knowledge and talking to other relevant people you will be drawing predominantly on informal theory. This theory becomes formal theory when it has been subjected to a more systematic study – for example, you may test out another detached worker's theory of how to work with young people in their own territory or you may draw on theory which helps you to understand the context of the young people – their role in society, their psychological and educational development. In considering how to use theory you will be looking for information about the nature of the 'problem' you are dealing with and the best way of achieving your desired outcome for the young people, the community and maybe even society in general. You will want to reach a conclusion about which approach works best and why.

The 'ingredients' of theory development

The end of the last section brought us to the point of looking at the general basis for theory development – *information and conclusions*.

Theories are only as good, applicable, useful, relevant, inspiring and creative as the information they are based on. This will take us into the general area of collecting evidence which is closely aligned with doing research. Needless to say there are different theories about how to conduct research and they have changed quite significantly over time too (more about this later).

ACTIVITY 1.5

Looking at our earlier practical 'problem' of young people gathering, what methods could be used to get more information to help you really understand the situation? Try to be as creative as you can and think of as many sources of information as possible.

Of course there are quite a number of different ways of starting this. You might have begun to get a background picture by using information that was already available in some format or other – you could have used 'secondary' sources such as reports and statistics. Another starting point might have been to check some of the issues out yourself, that is, you were thinking of using 'primary' data. Which different angles did you take on this? Maybe you wanted to know something about the actual scale of the issue, such as how many young people are actually gathering? Are they there all day or just in the evenings? Are they there every night or just on some nights? How old are they? Are they all from the local area? Are they all male, all female or is it a mixed gender group?

You might also be interested in understanding more about the nature of the issue – you might emphasise the qualitative angle of data collection. What does the shopkeeper mean by 'intimidation'? What are the young people actually doing? Has the shopkeeper really had any complaints? About what in particular? What are the concerns of the people who are anxious about the young people being there? Have there been any real incidents? When did this all start? What is the young people's take on all of this? How do they feel about the complaints? Are they happy with the current situation? What are their thoughts and views about their local neighbourhood?

It is quite likely that you have come up with an even longer list of more and different questions, and looking at the different methods you could use to find the answers could be even longer still. You could read professional journals, look at government reports, examine statistics, conduct surveys, issue questionnaires, carry out interviews (individually or in groups) and observe what is going on.

This chapter cannot explore the process of research in depth, but what we wish to emphasise is that the development of theory is both a rigorous and creative process, one that requires an open mind and a logical approach. However, it is important to draw attention to the fact that the theoretical base for research has undergone a significant shift over the past 40 years or so which is often captured under the move from 'positivist' thinking to 'post-positivist' thinking. Positivism viewed research as an objective exercise that aimed to explain or predict measurable and observable phenomena. For example, you could collect information about the social background of young people who commit crime and use this information to predict which young people are likely to commit crime in the future. This approach usually requires the information to be reduced to a numerical form so that statistical analysis can be used to make predictions. The positivist approach has its roots in science and assumes that there are social facts. Many would take issue with this and in relation to the example we have used would want to argue that the relationship between social background and crime is actually much more complex and that other factors such as family background, definition of what constitutes crime, economic circumstances, access to education are much more important in helping us to understand the relationship between crime and social background. Post-positivist thinking makes more room for multiple realities and approaches that acknowledge and capture many of the more subjective and exploratory aspects of investigating the lived world. Zena O'Leary (2004, pp4–7) outlines how this shift has affected all the assumptions about research; *the world* is portrayed less as predictable and controllable, but more as consisting of multiple realities; *the nature of research* which legitimises other ways of knowing and promotes a more collaborative role of *the researcher* which acknowledges inherent subjectivities; *methods* that leave greater scope for inductive theory development and *findings* that can have intrinsic worth without the need to be generalisable.

Who makes theory?

How do theories come about? Who is involved in developing them?

ACTIVITY **1.6**

- *What are the social issues that are prioritised for funding within in the neighbourhood that you live or work in?*

- *Are there any groups of young people who might be targeted for particular forms of youth work interventions?*

- *Who makes these decisions?*

- *What is the expertise of those in whom society has invested these powers?*

- *Are there alternative views to 'what needs doing'?*

- *Why and how do we arrive at the social categories that become part of the dominant discourse in our work?*

How difficult or easy did you find the questions in Activity 1.6? You might have come up with a range of different answers. It is quite likely, however, that you have identified areas of work that you feel need developing but it would be very difficult to get funding for. Alternatively, local people you work with might have a different view about what it takes to regenerate the local neighbourhood, or indeed identify a different set of local issues. In short, you as a community and youth worker or the people you work with could have developed different theories to those that govern the allocation of your funds.

What does this raise about the development of theory? We suggest that this raises two issues.

1. Who has the 'expertise' to develop theory?

2. On the basis of which data and information is theory developed?

Looking at how theories are developed and who is involved in the making of them takes us to the writing of Bourdieu (1992) and his concept of symbolic power. The process of shaping and defining reality is not one in which people take part in equal measure. Some people and groups/categories of people are given the power to make judgements and their voices will carry more weight than others' voices, and for many of these people society officially sanctions their status. For example, your university lecturer is given the legitimate power to decide what is a good or bad piece of writing, the police can deprive you of your liberty, and doctors can certify you as ill – regardless of how you actually feel yourself. What we have here is a generally accepted division of lay people and experts; the judgements of the latter can even have legal status, whereas the opinions of the former will not usually carry much weight outside fairly restricted situations. In many cases these divisions remain unchallenged, for example few would question the advice of a structural engineer when declaring a building safe or unsafe. Other areas of expertise, though, may be much more contested. In medicine, for example, women have challenged a dominant male perspective on women's health, and mental health too has been examined with regard to cultural bias and the social construction of sanity/insanity. When it comes to passing judgement on reality and the resulting theories to explain it, these distinctions become even more blurred.

Looking again in more detail at community and youth work, defining legitimate expertise can become quite tricky. The symbolic power that Bourdieu refers to can be observed in the way the judgement of certain groups of professionals is valued differently from the expertise of, for example, local people or young people. Although government policy relies heavily on the active involvement of local people in decision making at strategic levels it is important to look at the different ways 'expertise' can be handled in this context. As Burns et al. (2004) point out, community participation is not the same as consultation, although the terms are sometimes used loosely and interchangeably. What can often be observed is that local or alternative expertise becomes subsumed into a preset agenda that has largely been shaped by external expertise. The value of expertise is therefore closely bound up with (unequal) power relationships. A good example of this can be found in the introduction to the government's White Paper *Communities in Control*.

> *Community empowerment is the process of enabling people to shape and choose the services they use on a personal basis, so that they can influence the way those services are delivered.* (Department for Communities and Local Government, 2008, 13.1)

Many would disagree with this definition of community empowerment; it restricts the role of citizens to influencing the delivery of services rather than becoming involved in the level or type of service provision. This definition of empowerment is at odds with many that have

17

been developed as a consequence of research and reflections on practice which have led to a theory of empowerment which is concerned with individuals and groups gaining power and access to resources to take control of their own lives. This theory recognises that there is inequality and that the empowerment is concerned with changing the balance of power. Thus we can see that the policy makers choose to base their policies on research which fits with their ideology. Some theories are not taken into account even though they may be supported with an impressive range of evidence. However, what about people who are subjected to the policy, how are their theories taken into account?

As has been mentioned above theories need to be supported by evidence. The kind of evidence that will be acceptable, however, is also governed by issues of power. One of the main criticisms of a positivist research paradigm, for example, relates to the presumed 'neutrality' of knowledge. Moreover, it limits the way evidence can be collected and what is regarded as evidence. Feminist historians, for example, have drawn attention to the fact that research that relies primarily on written accounts will make it very difficult to account for the experience of women as history is predominantly recorded from the perspective of men's experience. This raises important issues of what is regarded as subjectivity and objectivity. Maria Mies (1993, p68) suggests that traditional research relationships are generally categorised as 'views from above' and need to be replaced by a 'view from below'. Otherwise, she argues, underprivileged groups will continue to be researched by more powerful elites who will also have the power to interpret the results through their particular perspectives. One of the fundamental aspects of critical social theory is therefore concerned with challenging the assumed neutrality and the prerogative of academic elites to shape and develop theory.

CHAPTER REVIEW

In the introduction to this chapter we raised the issue of the relevance of theory and the tensions which are often expressed about 'doing' versus 'thinking'. We have argued that one cannot exist without the other and indeed there would be no practice without reference to theory. However, we have also established that there are different degrees of 'usefulness' of different theoretical approaches, depending on what our standpoint is and what we want to achieve. Moreover, we have looked at the basis and foundations of theory development and the value of different forms of evidence. In doing so we cannot avoid raising the issue of power and how it permeates all aspects of the development and application of theory.

A separation of theory and practice is itself a reflection on a division of labour in line with the conflict theories outlined in Chapter 2, where the intellectual academic researchers are holding the power as the owners of knowledge, whereas the workers provide the raw material for the production of this knowledge and then are called upon to apply the resulting theories. In this sense community and youth workers sometimes reject theory on the basis that they are challenging the power of elites or intellectuals to define their reality. In this chapter we argue that this challenge to the elite needs to be matched with a claim to the right to being actively involved in the process of theory development. Not only is engaging with theory a crucial tool for empowerment and emancipation (as we discuss in more detail with reference to curriculum interests in Chapter 4), but also it is the mark of being a 'professional' as opposed to being a 'technician'.

FURTHER READING

Mies, M (1993) 'Towards a methodology for feminist research' in Hammersley, M (ed) *Social research, philosophy, politics and practice*. London: Sage.

Good overview of a feminist perspective on conducting research.

Mintzberg, H (2005) 'Developing theory about the development of theory' in Smith, KG and Hitt, MA, *Great minds in management*. Oxford: Oxford University Press.

Excellent, easy to read take on theory development.

Oko, J (2008) *Understanding and using theory in social work*. Exeter: Learning Matters.

Good further reading on using theory in the social professions, particularly useful with regard to the use of informal theory.

USEFUL WEBSITE

Jean Spence, 'In defence of youth work'. Leeds: 10 July 2009.

http://indefenceofyouthwork.wordpress.com/2009/08/19/in-defence-of-intellectually-rigorous-youth-work/

Chapter 2
Using social theory

Chris Parkin

CHAPTER OBJECTIVES

This chapter will help you meet the following National Occupational Standards.

1.1.5 Support young people in taking action and to tackle problems

2.3.2 Develop a culture and systems that promote equality and value diversity

3.2.1 Engage with the local community

4.1.1 Investigate the needs of young people and the community in relation to youth work

It will also introduce you to the following academic standards as set out in the youth and community work benchmark statement (2009, QAA).

7.1
- Contextualise the practice of youth work, community education and community development in society and policy.
- Question and be prepared to deconstruct taken for granted and common sense professional understandings.

7.2
- Create and apply theories about practice and demonstrate practice skills outlined in the benchmark statement.

Introduction

This chapter will help you to see why an understanding of social theory is relevant to your practice as a youth or community worker. It will look at the range of social theory and help you to develop a framework which will help you apply theory to practice and use your practice to understand theory. It is relatively easy to relate theory to practice in a mechanistic way without developing a critical understanding of theory – this chapter aims to move beyond this and equip you to engage with theory by having confidence in your understanding of practice in terms of social theory.

The chapter will introduce you to a range of social theories before considering the way in which theory explains communities and the way in which power operates in society. In each case we begin with an exercise that encourages you to think about your 'theories' of society, power, etc. There are two reasons for this: first, it helps you to start thinking about the issues that the theorists are grappling with; and second, it helps you to recognise that theorists have different explanations which are based on their experiences of the world.

Why is an understanding of social theory needed?

To understand why social theory is important we need to consider why community and youth work happens – why is it funded? Why do people get together to do things for their community and for young people? In part the answers to these questions depend on how we understand the society in which we live. There is a huge body of theory which is devoted to understanding 'society', and understanding it will help us understand the purpose of our work and how to make our practice effective.

It is important to start by thinking about what we mean by society; it's a word which is used frequently but what does it really mean. Is it a neighbourhood, a country; or both of these? Spend a few minutes thinking about what you mean by society – you could try drawing a picture. It would be a good idea to get other students to do the same and compare your pictures and then come up with a collective definition of society.

Some themes are likely to emerge – for example, does your picture have people in it? Are there any buildings? Churches? Mosques? Town halls? Schools? Community centres? Hospitals? Police stations? Now try to come up with your own definition of what society is. Please don't reach for the sociological dictionary at this point – it's important to start with your own views.

Here are some examples of definitions that you may come up with.

- Society is a term that describes the collection of people and institutions which impact on what I and other people can and can't do.

- Society is a term that describes the relationships between people.

Most of our definitions will imply that there is a relationship between society and the way in which people behave, so it is important to consider what motivates people to behave in certain ways. One way of doing this is to consider whether people have an innate tendency to be co-operative, helpful and kind individuals (good), or are selfish, obstructive and nasty (bad). Most people find this a very difficult task – they don't want to think about people being always bad or always good, but it is often helpful to try to polarise situations. Our understanding of society will depend on whether we think people want to co-operate and get on with each other rather than fight and grab the goodies for themselves.

What do you think about the nature of individuals and what evidence do you have for this?

Theorists have different ways of thinking about the relationship between individuals and society.

ACTIVITY **2.1**

Which of these statements matches your thoughts about society? What kinds of assumptions do you think these statements make about the nature of individuals? You may find it difficult to choose – make a note of which bits of each statement you agree or disagree with and why.

Statement 1 Society is like a human body. Each of its parts is linked to form a whole. Disharmony is evidence of disease and should be treated. Problems are the result of individual failing and people need 'treatment'.

Statement 2 Society is made up of lots of different groups and individuals, each of whom is as worthy as each other and potentially as equal as the other. The majority work together to create harmony; disharmony and social problems are the result of a malfunction in the system.

Statement 3 Society comprises opposing interest groups all pursuing their own needs which are fundamentally contradictory. These groups constantly clash and social existence is a series of power struggles. Social problems and disharmony are the result of this power struggle.

Statement 4 Society comprises self-seeking individuals. Each individual pursues their own best interests and in so doing works towards the better good of society. Social problems and disharmony are the result of the limitation of individual freedom or individual evil.

This activity has begun to engage you in the questions that social theorists engage with: What is society? What is the relationship between individuals and society? You have begun to develop your own theory of society; remember that social theory in its simplest form is just someone else's idea of what society is and how it works. Often social theory seems to be very complex and difficult to understand; this is usually because society itself is complex. Try sharing the results of the above exercise with your colleagues or peers; you will probably find that you have chosen different statements or even the same statements for different reasons. It would be surprising if you agreed with each other because you are basing your views on your own experiences of society and relationships with other people. This demonstrates that when you are engaged with social theory you are not working with absolutes – there are different opinions based on the same facts or observations. Later in this chapter we will explore how these facts and observations are collected.

In community and youth work there is often a tension between helping and supporting individuals, enabling them to function in society by developing their personal and social selves, and helping individuals and groups to change society to better meet their personal and social needs. Your views on which of these tasks you are engaged in, or at least the balance you try to achieve between these tasks and the way in which you implement them, will depend on how you think society works. A key issue in social theory is the relationship between individuals and society. Does society enable or restrict individual development? Or is society the product of individual effort and relationships? In the next section we will look at a range of social theorists and examine their views on society.

When considering the work of theorists it is important to consider the context of their theories. For example, the early theorists were attempting to make sense of a world undergoing considerable change due to industrialisation. Theorists in the mid-twentieth century were concerned with the role of new forms of communication linked to media and the ease of transportation. Current theorists are influenced by globalisation, the nature of power and post-industrialism.

Social theorists

Social theorists are concerned with both the nature of society and the methods by which we can investigate it, and theories tend to fall into one of the following categories.

- **Macro sociology or structural perspectives**

  Focus is on the social system, the way that society as a whole fits together. Methods used to find out about society tend to be focused on the gathering of social facts.

- **Micro sociology or social action perspectives**

  Society is the product of human activity, and focuses on individuals and interpersonal relations. Methods used to find out about society tend to focus on discovering individuals' interpretation of their social life.

Please note that this is a simplification. Some theorists use both these approaches and argue that this is necessary to gain a complete understanding of social processes. A note of caution: although many theorists present their ideas as if they were mutually exclusive, their works overlap; many of them were and are engaged in continual debate with colleagues and sometimes their thoughts are based on the findings of previous theorists – perhaps re-examined in the light of changes in society or application of theory to a different topic.

The following pages will outline in fairly simplistic terms a summary of some of the key theorists in order to provide an overview of the theories. This is not a sociology text book and it is essential that you use one of the text books listed in the bibliography or some of the web links suggested to aid your understanding of these theorists. My intention here is to introduce you to some of the key concepts which underpin social theory to help you make sense of your reading. You will need to consider how useful these theories are in helping you make sense of your role as a community and youth worker. For example how do they help you to understand why a young person doesn't want to attend school, why they take drugs, get pregnant, get into offending behaviour or even how young people learn to become citizens in society.

The development of the discipline known as sociology took place during the early part of the nineteenth century and Auguste Compte is generally accredited with the discipline, though we must remember that this was not the first time that learned scholars concerned themselves with the nature of society. Early philosophers such as Aristotle and Plato began to investigate the political organisation of Greek communities and apply this to domestic and commercial activities in the first century AD. For example Scott (2006) draws our attention to Ibu Khaldun, a Muslim scholar who in 1377 used Aristotelian ideas to explore the conditions under which strong states could resolve social conflicts.

Auguste Compte viewed society as a self-contained reality which functions as an integrated whole. He termed his philosophy positivism. He thought that it was possible to discover social facts in a similar way to the discovery of scientific knowledge and thus knowledge about the social world could be used to predict the likely results of different policies concerned with social life. Most of the early theorists who followed tended to develop this approach, attempting to uncover rules of social life in order to predict changes or the impact of developments such as industrialisation, war, migration, education, etc.

Macro sociology/structural theory

Macro or structural theories focus on social systems – based on an organic model of society which sees society as a whole, with things which happen being explicable in terms of their contribution to the survival of the social system. This group of theories suggests that the explanation for human behaviour cannot be found in the experience of the individual and that objective forces beyond our control have to be uncovered and examined. These forces can be found in the systems of language and in the ideological and political structures of society. Within structural theories there are two main perspectives: those based on consensus; and those based on conflict.

Consensus

Within consensus theories there is an assumption of shared values. Functionalism is the main consensus theory. An easy way to understand this theory is to compare society to a human body with the various structures in society having specific functions. For example the family could be seen to be the function that regulates reproduction, the church has the function of promoting and upholding moral values, the legal system regulates society, the economic system is the function which provides food and shelter and so on.

Durkheim 1893–1917
A good example of this consensus can be found within the theories of Durkheim, who is a functionalist. Like many early sociologists, Durkheim considers the changes in society brought about by industrialisation. He identifies the concepts of social solidarity and argues that in pre-industrial societies social solidarity was mechanical – based on similarities between individuals who generally shared the same roles, beliefs and values (Haralambos et al., 2004). In industrial society social solidarity was organic – and relied on differences. In order to produce goods, housing and social life individuals specialised in different roles and this required co-operation. *This organic solidarity is achieved whenever a complex division of labour and high levels of individualism are associated with a moral regulation of contractual and exchange relations and of relations among different occupations* (Scott, 2006, p56).

Durkheim argued that the workings of social systems are not always apparent to the individuals within the system. His work on suicide demonstrated his belief that social characteristics are the main determinant of behaviour rather than any individual motivation.

Talcott Parsons 1902–1979

Functionalism enjoyed a revival in the 1930s–1960s. It built on the work of anthropologists who study human evolution. Parsons identified that societies required four functional prerequisites or needs in order to operate. Thus the structures of systems in society were made explicit by Parsons. These functions are as follows.

- **Adaptation**: Process by which society caters for its members' physical needs, e.g. food, shelter. Part of the system which generates material resources necessary for continuation of society, i.e. the economic systems.

- **Goal attainment**: Process by which agreed social priorities are established and activities co-ordinated to achieve ends – political systems.

- **Integration**: Process to reduce conflict by setting up norms and rules, for example, religion, laws, the legal system.

- **Pattern maintenance**: Latency process of socialisation understanding and desire to conform to norms – leisure to restore, energise and enthuse its members.

(Adapted from Worsley, 1988, pp474–5)

Parsons thus identified how social institutions were formed and he considered how they operated. He emphasised the importance of a common value system in maintaining social order. Robert Merton, who was a contemporary of Parsons, developed this work by demonstrating that society could also have dysfunctions. Functions can have unintended consequences which can be dysfunctional, for example welfare provisions designed to meet the needs of the population during periods of unemployment or sickness can create a dependency.

Conflict

Conflict theorists argue that society consists of groups with different interests, these differences are a constant feature of society and they are reproduced in all aspects of social systems. There are many conflict theories – Marxism and feminism are examples, as is the work of Bourdieu and Gramsci, which is discussed in the chapter on educational theory.

Marxism

Marxism is a theoretical perspective that takes its name from the German-born scholar who wrote extensively on philosophy, economics and sociology; his work has been interpreted in many ways by subsequent theorists. In essence Marx argues that the economic system is the key determinant of social systems. He tends to agree with functionalists in that there are various structures in society but argues that it is the economic structure which determines social relationships and that all other structures or functions are shaped by the economic structure. He termed the economic system **infrastructure** and the other aspects of society the **superstructure**. Marx argues that there is an inherent conflict between the forces of production – that is, owners of land, raw material and machinery and those who provide labour. The owners of the means of production aim to gain the highest profit from their production which means that it is in their interests to keep wages as low as possible. Marx argues that all other parts of the social system are related to the economic system. Thus the education system is geared to meeting the needs of the economy, and religion is an illusion – *the opium of the people . . . to dull the pain caused by oppression* (Marx in Bottomore and Rubel, 1963 cited in Haralambos et al., 2004, p409). He argued that the conflict between labour and the owners of the means of production would lead to the collapse of the economic system because the providers of labour would recognise their oppression, leading to protest and withdrawal of their labour. We can see then that Marx still adopted the functionalist approach but instead of a system based on consensus it was based on conflict.

Weber

Weber was a contemporary of Marx and he agreed with much of Marx's theory. However, he emphasised the need to see individuals as reasoning and motivated actors recognising that the individual's role in creating social and historical situations is central. He recognised that actions take place within a social context thus the economic systems are important but not the only factor. A key concept identified by Weber was **Verstehen**, which stresses that in order to understand the actions of individuals it is important to consider their intention. He identified some ideal types of behaviour: affective or emotional action which is the result of an individual emotional state; traditional action which is the result of habit; and rational action which is based on an awareness of the goal an individual wants to achieve. Weber's work informs the subsequent theorists who developed social action theory.

Feminism

Feminism is another example of a conflict theory, though there are many strands of feminism. In the case of feminism the source of the conflict is the exploitation of women. Society is dominated by patriarchal institutions. It is apparent from the outline of the early theorists in the preceding pages that sociological theory has been written from a male perspective. We have also commented on the way in which women's voices are marginalised in theory more generally in Chapter 1, Chapter 3 and Chapter 4.

There are many different perspectives within feminism, for example: radical feminism, Marxist/socialist feminism, Black feminism and Liberal feminism. These perspectives differ in terms of their view of the causes of gender inequality and the action required to overcome it. Radical feminists see 'men' as the cause of gender inequality and argue that radical change in the structures of society are needed to overcome the oppression of women. Marxist feminists see the capitalist system as the main cause of inequality, arguing that it is mainly the system which benefits from women's unpaid labour; like radical feminists they argue that the position of women can only be improved by change to the structures of society. Liberal feminists argue that both men and women are disadvantaged by gender inequalities and that it can be overcome by a process of gradual change. Examples include the introduction of the Sex Discrimination Act in 1975. Black feminists argue that the particular problems faced by black women are not addressed by either feminism or anti-racist campaigners. They argue that change will come about by drawing on the experiences of black women to counter the assumptions that inequalities are based on.

Micro sociology/social action theory

Social action theories suggest that the structure of society arises out of the actions of individuals. As we have seen, the distinction between social action theory and Structuralism is not always clear cut. Indeed, Durkheim's work is often cited by social action theorists and Weber made an important contribution to the development of interpretive social theory as a result of his consideration of social actions despite his belief that the economic system was the main determinant of social life. There are two main theoretical perspectives: symbolic interactionism and phenomenology. These are often referred to as interpretive sociology.

Symbolic interactionism

Symbolic interactionism is an approach which emerged from the writings of American sociologists and social psychologists in the 1920s and 1930s. It explains social actions in terms of the meaning that individuals give to them. It is based on a view that people develop their identities, understanding of society and ideas about fairness through their interactions with other people. The approach was initiated by Herbert Mead and developed by Herbert Blumer in 1969. Blumer was concerned about the process of social analysis and maintained that people act on the basis of the meanings attached to actions, human interaction is essential for the making of these meanings, the actions are subject to interpretation and consequently social networks and institutions are fluid and consequently being renegotiated. This approach was further developed by Erving Goffman who focused on the extent to which people act out roles depending on social situation. It is easy to observe this phenomenon. How often have you seen young people displaying one type of behaviour with their peers and another with their families or within a school setting? Many youth workers find this theory useful to explore young people's actions from a range of perspectives. Take, for example, a group of young people starting a fire in a derelict area – are they doing this because they have been collecting rubbish and think that the easiest way to get rid of it is to burn it away from residents so as not to cause a nuisance? Or are they homeless and seeking a way to keep warm? Or is it, perhaps, near bonfire night and they set the bonfire alight early? It is often important to explore the meaning behind actions.

Phenomenology

This approach was developed by Schutz, Berger and Luckman and the emphasis is on the human experience – how the mind works and how humans classify and make sense of their world. A significant development of this approach is **ethnomethodology** – a method of research which examines how people construct their social world. Ethnomethodology can be translated as 'people's methods'; Garfinkle (1967) developed this branch of sociology. He challenged the view that the social world we inhabit was a structured one. He focused on how people give meanings to and interpret behaviour and the methods used by people to communicate with each other.

Contempory social theory

There are many strands in contemporary social theory. Some have explored in more detail the extent to which individuals influence society arguing that society is formed through relationships between people. They therefore focus on analysing the actions of individuals and their impact on society. The work of Giddens in the latter part of the twentieth century has brought these two approaches together in his theory of structuration which acknowledges that *people make society but are also constrained by it* (Calhoun et al., 2007).

Other theorists identify themselves as post structuralist or post modernists and they have revisited the work of the earlier classical theorists in the light of current trends in society. Critical sociologists such as Foucault, Habermas and Bourdieu (referred to in Chapter 4) are examples of theorists who have developed Marxist theory, exploring in more detail the role of power in society. It is also worth noting that some contemporary theorists are classified as neo-Marxist signalling that they are adapting Marxist views to contemporary society – recognising changes to the nature of capital.

Engaging with social theory

You now need to consider what all this theory means for you as a community and youth worker. My argument is that as community and youth workers you are engaged in the social world and the purpose of your job is to help people achieve a good quality of life, either by action to change society to better meet their needs or by action to help individuals participate in the opportunities provided by society. To do this you need to understand society.

I want to emphasise here that theories are not necessarily right! This should be evident from the range of theories presented. Your task is to use theory to help you develop your own understanding of what society is and how it operates. You can achieve this in a number of ways.

ACTIVITY 2.2

- *Compare the theories to the definitions of society you came up with in Activity 2.1. Make a note of how your ideas of society fit with the theories.*

- *Choose theories that fit best with your idea. Now read about those theories in more detail using the texts listed at the end of the chapter. Make a note of any experiences you have that support the theory. Try to come up with real examples of social behaviour which you think fit the theory. This could be based on observations about the behaviour of young people or particular social groups or evidence of the way in which your life has been affected by social structures such as churches, government or the economy.*

- *Discuss your reading and examples with a fellow student or colleague, and try to identify the things you have differing opinions on and try to change each other's mind by presenting an argument.*

Community

In community and youth work our practice tends to take place in communities. It would therefore be useful to consider whether social theories help us to understand the context of communities.

ACTIVITY 2.3

Spend a few minutes thinking about what you understand by the term 'community'.

Look in some newspapers, magazines and text books, underline the word 'community' and then try to replace the word with another word that would still make sense.

Try to come up with a definition of community.

You will probably find that the word 'community' is used many different ways – for example, community policing, care in the community, community service, community consultation, Muslim community, gay community etc. Below are some definitions you might have come up with. Is your definition there?

Possible definitions of community

- Community is a group of people who have lived the same way for a long time and don't like newcomers changing this.
- Personal sense of belonging to a wider group in society which supports the common values and interests of individuals.
- People who are active make up a community.
- A nice friendly word that indicates common bonds of interaction of a certain group of people.
- Community means a gathering of a small group of people having something in common; lifestyle, family, class etc.
- A community is where everybody knows each other, all pull together in times of crisis; it is somewhere that all the people have access to the amenities that are available to them, and where there is a spirit of community.
- It's where a group of people all come together probably sharing some things in common. For example sometimes a community is formed when there has been a tragedy.
- Friendly attitude, sharing thoughts, practising culture. A bunch of people with a friendly attitude.
- Community is a place where I feel I belong, feel safe. The community is a group of people who have something in common.
- A community is a place or a town or a city etc., where a group of people conform to a set of guidelines or rules, so that they all have something in common; people who do not fit this bill are often pushed out of the community.

- A collection of people and values identified with an area, group or cause with provision for conflict and division.

- A group, team, collection of people who belong to the same geographical area, share the area's facilities and contribute to the area.

There are some common themes in these definitions:

- sense of belonging;

- common interests and/or values;

- geographical area;

- relationship network – families.

There are also some views expressed about whether community is a positive or negative concept. We are now going to look at what social theories have to say about community.

Concepts of community

As we have seen it is extremely difficult to pinpoint a definition of community. An examination of the concept of community in social theory demonstrates that the term is so contested it has almost been considered to be a useless concept. In fact, a look in some of the more recent sociology text books will reveal that the body of theory linked to community is often completely missing! In reality much current theory related to community is found within the theories of urban and political geography (see Lees, 2004; DeFillippis and Saegert, 2007).

In 1955 Hillery reviewed 94 definitions of community and concluded the only thing they had in common was that they all referred to people. However, he went on to classify three broad types of definition:

- type of relationship;

- locality;

- local social system.

Generally in sociology the focus has been on the latter two types of definition, but in planning and geography the focus is usually on locality. This contributes to the confusion of the term. Despite the confusions surrounding the term 'community' these three types of definition remain useful as they encompass the ways in which the term is used in both traditional and current theoretical perspectives. It is important to remember that theory which tries to explain society also applies to community – the general approaches outlined in the previous chapter apply equally to communities.

A key feature of almost all theorists who are concerned with community is that their starting point is usually that community is breaking down and that this has a negative impact on all aspects of society. The following section will outline the ways in which the different types of community have been considered by social theorists.

Type of relationship

A sense of shared identity; this definition corresponds most closely with the colloquial use of the term – idea of a spirit of community, sense of communality.

This definition need have no geographical basis – for example, Muslim community, scientific community, gay community, deaf community. It may also exist between people who have never met each other. Many of the early theorists focused on community as a type of relationship; they tend to use community as a critique of urban industrialisation. This provides an example of how empirical descriptions (studies of communities as they are) can be influences of normative prescriptions (expressions of values about what community life should be like).

One of the most influential nineteenth-century writers on community was Ferdinand Tönnies and his ideas remain influential today. He focused on community as a type of relationship. In 1887 he identified two types of community: 'Gemeinschaft' and 'Gesellschaft'. These are types of relationship, *not* settlement patterns.

Gemeinschaft roughly translates as 'community' and by this Tönnies meant that:

- relationships were close and based on face to face contacts;
- status was ascribed;
- people identify with the community's homogeneous culture reinforced by moral custodians, e.g. church and the family;
- kinship is of fundamental importance.

Gesellschaft roughly translates as 'association'; it consists of everything that community is not, for example:

- relationships are impersonal and formal;
- status is achieved;
- individuality is stressed;
- people divide into subcultures.

Tönnies used these concepts to make sense of the changes sweeping across Europe and he used the concepts in relation to social relationships not locality. Subsequent writers have shifted the emphasis to classifying kinds of community.

Locality

Locality is a geographical expression denoting a human settlement located within a particular local territory. It is used most in urban sociology texts in the first half of the twentieth century (see Simmel, Wirth and Pahl in Worsley 1988). This idea regained popularity in the late 1980s – for example, Doreen Massey (1984) David Byrne (1989) who identified locale as an important component in understanding society. The idea is that there is something about the physical environment which impacts on social systems – this is a structuralist approach but it also employs social action techniques by examining the meanings that people give to their locality.

Georg Simmel related Tönnies' work to specific localities in his 1903 essay 'The Metropolis and mental life' (Worsley 1988). He was concerned with the impact that industrial life had on the mental state of the population and he was clearly hostile to the process of industrialisation and mechanisation. He characterised urban life as:

- rational as opposed to rural life which is based on feelings and emotional relationships;

- based on a money economy which encourages a matter of fact treatment of people and things so that social relationships become impersonal and standardised;

- impersonal which leads to an inability to distinguish individuality;

- isolated – a lack of face to face contact results in a formal reserve thus individuals become isolated from each other.

He believed that these factors led to the individual becoming estranged from other members of urban society and other social groups. This analysis has similarities with Durkheim's notions of organic solidarity.

This approach to urbanism culminated in a classic paper by the Chicago sociologist Louis Wirth in his paper 'Urbanism as a Way of Life' in 1938 (in Worsley, 1988, p243). His paper concerned the process of moving from the country to the city. He defined a city as 'a relatively large dense and permanent settlement of socially heterogeneous individuals'.

He went on to identify the major characteristics which define a city:

- size of population;

- density;

- degree of homogeneity.

These factors explain the characteristics of urban life and account for the differences between cities of various types and sizes.

Thus size leads to roads, public transport and prevents everyone from knowing each other as demonstrated by the relationship between a taxi driver and his fare.

Density leads to traffic congestion, housing shortages and differences between the population become visible – mutual exploitation is encouraged. He drew attention to the likely rise in social and interpersonal conflict by frequent physical contact but decreasingly meaningful social contact.

Heterogeneity leads to a more diverse and specialised population so the class structure becomes more complicated and opaque – individuals no longer know their place.

Essentially sociologists such as Wirth and Simmel were developing a classification of communities based on a rural urban continuum and suggesting that social relationships were dependent on the physical structure of communities. These ideas about community as a locality were taken up by a number of British sociologists in a tradition of community studies which emerged in the UK during the 1950s and 1960s (Bell and Newby, 1971). These studies drew on anthropology with the researchers spending time collecting data in a range of towns and villages. Sociologists such as Wilmott and Young explored urban neighbourhoods and found that they exhibited the characteristics of settlements that should have been at the rural end of the continuum (Worsley, 1988, p251). Some of the key findings of these studies were:

- increasing urbanisation and move to towns had not destroyed community;

- dispute about the nature of community;

- geographical determinism – the idea that spaces could be designed to foster a sense of community which led to housing estates being designed to create private and communal space.

Some felt that while these studies were rich in detail (empirically rich) they were flawed in that they were not located within a wider context of social change or structural inequality (theoretically barren) (see Crow and Allan 1994 pp13–14).

A number of subsequent studies – Rex and Moore (1967), Gans (1962), Pahl (1966) and Stacey (1969) – questioned the extent to which locality influenced the way in which one lives, having discovered that social class, housing policies and other 'constraints of choice' were far more important. This led to a question of whether localities really mattered given that they are not self-sustaining or autonomous social systems.

Margaret Stacey (1969) in her article 'The Myth of Community Studies' argued that the concept of community had taken on meanings which were not analytically valid. She demonstrated that it was not possible to provide any reliable definition of either a *defined geographical area or the boundaries of the group in which the sense of community was said to reside* (Stacey, 1969, pp134–47).

At this point the attention given to communities as localities by social theorists declined. An examination of sociological literature demonstrates that by the late 1970s the concept of community or community studies was paid scant attention by social theorists. Indeed, current editions of popular social theory text books such as Haralambos et al. (2004), Macionis (2007) and Giddens (2006) make no mention of the sociology of community. More recently it has been picked up by urban sociologists and geographers (Hoggett, 1997) who have become more interested in the relationship between locality and local social systems.

Local social systems

In this sense community is viewed as a set of social relationships, which take place within a locality. Thus a community in this sense may be said to exist when a network of inter-relationships is established between those people living in the same locality. The relationships are not necessarily harmonious, they can be based on conflict; the key issue is that the relationships exist.

This idea of community as a social system has recently gained much credibility through the work of theorists examining the concept of social capital. Putnam (2000) has popularised this concept and as a result there can be little doubt that the notion of community, whether or not it can be adequately defined in sociological terms, has much currency in current policy initiatives and the practice of community and youth work.

The concept of community has been a key feature of New Labour Policy:

> At the heart of my beliefs is the idea of community. I don't just mean the local villages, towns and cities in which we live. I mean that our fulfilment as individuals lies in a decent society of others. My argument . . . is that the renewal of community is the answer to the challenges of a changing world.
>
> (Tony Blair quoted in Levitas, 2000, p189)

This reference to community is based on an understanding of community as a social system. There are many interrelated concepts that influence current community policy in the UK – civic society, social capital and communitarianism. The debate about what a community is, whether it is a real or imagined concept and whether it is a good or bad thing remains as central to contemporary theory as it was to previous theorists. The distinction about whether community is a geographical space/locality or a set of social relationships/networks remains though there is some recognition of the interrelated nature of locality and relationships and the focus is on social networks as illustrated by the emphasis on social capital. Theorists tend to consider the extent to which social networks either create or restrict access to economic capital and this has implications on whether communities are seen as good or bad.

Theorists exploring the concept of social capital tend to use two types of approach which can be linked to the distinction between consensus theory and conflict theory outlined in the section on social theory.

Although the concept of social capital has been popularised by Putnam it was used in earlier writing. Loury (1977 in DeFillippis, 2001) used the term 'social capital' to explain the consequence of social position in gaining access to individual success. His basic assumption was that *the social context within which individual maturation occurs strongly conditions what otherwise competent individuals can achieve*. Thus a young person living in a poor area with limited access to resources is generally unable to access the same quality of education as a young person in a wealthy area with access to income because not only are the schools likely to provide a better quality of education but they will also have a choice of alternative forms of education. He takes this argument further and points out that even if a young person succeeds in the school in a poorer area they will not have made the same connections with people of a higher status who are well connected. In other words he used social capital to refer to the commonly used statement – it's not what you know, it's who you know. He recognised that this type of social relationship worked at all levels – for example, social connections in some areas are likely to give individuals access to goods via an alternative economy.

A French sociologist, Pierre Bourdieu, developed this use of social capital as *an explicit attempt to understand the production of classes and class divisions* (Bourdieu in DeFillippis, 2001). Thus Bourdieu conceives of social capital as connected to economic capital and linked to a set of power relations. In other words he adopts a conflictual perspective – social networks will be used by individuals to gain advantage and consequently they will try to prevent others from gaining access to these resources. He defines social capital as something which exists within social networks which can be realised by individuals rather than simply a product of social networks (see Chapter 4).

Putnam's definition of social capital is different. He equates social capital with social networks and in particular the extent of voluntary organisations which people belong to within a given locality. He suggested that individuals and groups can possess or not possess social capital and that group or community social capital can be measured by adding up the extent of individual social capital as measured by membership of social networks. He adopts a consensus view of communities arguing that the existence of social capital implies trust between individuals.

Putnam suggests that the amount of social capital within a community can be measured by the number of voluntary organisations within it and that high levels of social capital will result in improved development of economic capital. It is perhaps for this reason that his ideas have been used by UK and American politicians and the World Bank. DeFillippis (2007) among others has challenged this assumption pointing out that even using Putnam's own measures of social capital areas with high social capital are not prosperous economically and some areas with low social capital such as gated communities in parts of America are very prosperous economically. Putnam is further criticised for failing to recognise the way in which social networks are influenced by external factors – for example, bank-lending policies, social housing policy and immigration policies.

In reality both theorists and individuals have tended to run all three definitions of community together. Look at the list of definitions that the students identified earlier and look again at the definition you came up with – you are likely to find that you included aspects of all three types of community. There has been an assumption that life in a particular locality promotes a structure of relationships that result in the presence or absence of a sense of community. There has also been a tendency to assume that rural areas consist of closely knit inhabitants living in happy communion while in cities there are only isolated lonely individuals lacking any sense of mutual identity. This leads to the assumption that communities are a good thing – with little attention being paid to the negative aspects of communities – for example the way in which communities can be exclusive and hostile to newcomers.

Practical use of theory

A commonly used exercise in the practice of community and youth work is to produce a community profile. These are often useful for workers to understand the context of their practice. However the information you gather in completing a community profile needs to be analysed in terms of what it tells you about the characteristics of the community and your role within it; you will need to draw on theory to do this. There are many publications that will help you to construct a community profile and some of these are listed at the end of the chapter.

In general terms constructing a community profile will require you to respond to the following questions.

- What are the boundaries of the community? Are the administrative boundaries of geographical communities the same as the boundaries that local residents would identify with? How do you establish boundaries for a community of interest?

- What is the population of the community like?

- What kind of social structures are there and to what extent are these controlled by the community, e.g. schools, shops, industry, religious organisations, leisure activities, housing, legal systems (police, courts).

- The extent of consensus and conflict in the community with evidence of how this is demonstrated.

Look at the following case study which is a brief summary of a community profile for a geographical community and try to use the theories outlined in this chapter to work out what the issues are in the community and how you would respond to these issues as a youth or community worker.

Below are some questions relevant to the practice of community and youth work.

- Should communities be considered as a social structure?

- What is their relationship to the economic system?

- What impact, if any, do communities have on individuals and social relationships?

- To what extent is your role to build on the social networks in communities or attempt to change them?

CASE STUDY

Community profile for a geographical community

Area

This is an inner city neighbourhood which has had some regeneration funding which is now coming to an end. It is a traditional working class area with a history of shipbuilding and heavy industry which is now almost non existent. The area includes student accommodation and a major hospital. The boundaries of the area are unclear – the area which people identify with is split by local government ward boundaries.

Population

Predominantly white (92 per cent) with a small Bangladeshi community concentrated in a few streets. There has been a recent influx of Filipino and Indian hospital workers living in private rented accommodation. There are also a number of refugees and asylum seekers who have settled in the area as a result of the dispersal programme.

Community facilities

- *Churches – Catholic, Anglican and Salvation Army: the Catholic Church has a social club and the other churches have community rooms with activities provided by church members.*

- *Community centre providing dancing, carpet bowls, judo and senior citizens activities. No paid staff other than cleaning and maintenance.*

- *An independent citywide black and minority ethnic (BME) project providing advice – staffed by one development worker and volunteers funded totally by trust funds.*

- *An independent youth project managed by local people providing detached sessions, weekly discos and a junior club. Some educational provision is also provided – such as computer courses.*

- *A community development project funded from trusts and contracts which has developed a number of smaller groups in response to community needs. This project is struggling to secure long-term funding.*

- *Shopping facilities – a traditional high street which is becoming run down. A small out of town retail park on the edge of the area.*

- *Good public transport links.*

- *Good health facilities – GP surgeries, hospital and dental surgeries.*

- *No central or local government offices.*

- *Three primary schools including one Catholic school. No secondary school.*

- *The area has a mix of housing about a third each of owner occupied, private rented and social housing. Property prices are low.*

You will probably find you used more than one theory. A functionalist perspective may have helped you in considering the social structures in the community. In particular you may have identified the absence of a secondary school and the impact that this will have on the community. If you developed this analysis further you may have drawn on Talcott Parsons functions earlier and identified that there appear to be systems for 'pattern maintenance' with a strong network of churches and community projects. Alternatively you may have drawn on conflict theory and identified that the area had originally developed to house workers for the economic system and now that the economy no longer requires these traditional industries there is no function for this community. In looking at theory linked to communities you may have thought of the area as a local social system.

It is likely that you found it difficult to use some theories without having more information; the case study does not include any qualitative information so you have little understanding about what it is like to live in the area. It may be that local residents are concerned about the influx of Filipino and Indian workers in terms of the capacity of local services. It is likely that there will be some issues linked to understanding the different cultures in the area and the integration of the newcomers – drawing on interpretive theories might be useful here as they may help you to understand the meaning behind individual actions. In considering your role as a worker I guess you found the lack of detail about what residents thought very frustrating. For example, if you knew that there was some resentment of students who exhibit rowdy behaviour and make little, if any, contribution to community life this may help you to think about the purpose of your practice. However, you would still need to draw on theory. It may be that you would think about the cause of the problems with students in functionalist terms – there are too many students and the facilities in the area are not adequate – the solution is to work towards improving facilities or reduce the numbers of students. Alternatively you may draw on interpretive theories and identify that there is a lack of understanding between the students and local residents and that the solution is to provide more opportunities for the students to meet residents in order to gain a better understanding. It may be that you could apply theories of social capital and promote the involvement of the students in community organisations.

It would now be useful for you to carry out your own community profile exercise or revisit one that you have carried out previously to identify how you can use theory to explore the issues you find.

Power in society

In the run through of social theory on the last few pages there have been a number of occasions where the role of power in society has been alluded to. We are now going to explore power in more detail. It is always a good idea to start with exploring what power means in your life – especially in relation to your practice as a community and youth worker.

ACTIVITY 2.4

- *Identify three times in your life when you have felt powerful.*

- *Identify three times in your life when you felt powerless or oppressed.*

- *Try to identify why you felt powerful or powerless and use these reasons to help you come up with a definition of power.*

Most people find this activity difficult. Get your colleagues to try the activity then try asking your boss or tutor to have a go. Do they find it any easier? You may come across some situations which seem almost the same yet one person feels powerful and another powerless.

You may find that you have associated power with physical or mental strength, status at work or within your family. Some people will have identified powerlessness in relation to poverty, race or gender but my guess is that few people will have identified themselves as powerful by reason of their gender, wealth or race! Why do you think this is? Often those in positions of power fail to recognise that they are powerful – this could be because they think that their experiences are normal. Thus you are unlikely to think that having access to education gives you any power but for many people education is restricted depending on their social status, gender or race.

Have a look at these examples that some students came up with.

- We feel powerful when in control, for example we are able to make decisions, are given responsibility which gives us a sense of achievement and self-worth.

- We feel powerless when we are unable to make a difference, for example when someone is dying or because we have no rights and are unable to make decisions. This makes us feel insignificant, weak, useless and angry.

- We feel oppressed when we are labelled, controlled and dictated to; this makes us feel abused and belittled.

We will now look at how power is explained in social theory. Social theories address dimensions and aspects of power.

- The social characteristics of the powerful and the powerless.

- The development of ideological frameworks that legitimise the exercise of power.

- The social effects or consequences of exercising of power.

- Who rules in society?

- How power is created, legitimised and reproduced?

The experiences that the students identified suggest that power is related to control. Power, almost by definition, involves the rule by the few over the majority and we have to understand the processes (structural and interpersonal) whereby power is legitimised.

As we have already seen, the different theories tend to consider power in different ways with some hardly considering it at all and others almost suggesting that society can't be understood without an analysis of power, relations. Functionalism for example as discussed by Talcott Parsons hardly considers power, but when he does his emphasis is on the overall capacity of a society not the dominance of some members by others (see Giddens 1967). Most consensus theories tend to view power as a mechanism making systems work, e.g. stratification systems like social class to ensure that the skills of the population are used effectively based on the assumption that the upper classes are better equipped to make decisions.

Alternatively, conflict theorists such as Marx view power as the key to understanding society, in particular the power of the owners of the means of production over the proletariat (providers of labour). A useful definition of power was developed by Weber (in Haralambos et al., 2004, p540), a conflict theorist who built on the work of Marx. He suggests that power is the ability to make people do what they wouldn't otherwise do. He considers different types of power.

Coercion: People forced to do as they are told under threat of punishment (for example, in a prison or a school classroom).

Authority – which can take the following forms.

- **Charismatic**: People obey because of the personal qualities of the person doing the telling. Well-known charismatic figures include Jesus Christ, Hitler and Chairman Mao. However, charismatic figures may arise in any social grouping and such people assume positions of authority over others on the basis of personal qualities of leadership perceived in that individual by other group members.

- **Traditional**: Those who exercise authority do so because they continue a tradition and support the preservation and continuation of existing values and social ties (for example, the Queen is Head of State in Britain, a position she inherited on the basis of traditional rules of succession for the monarchy).

- **Rational – legal**: Those in authority give orders (and expect to be obeyed) because the office they fill gives them the right to give orders. Anyone who fills the same position has the right to issue orders, which means that this type of authority is not based on the personal qualities of the individual. Orders are only to be obeyed if they are relevant to the situation in which they are given.

Weber's use of power relates to the way in which power operates at a structural level rather than considering power between individuals.

Lukes (1974) identified three dimensions of power after analysing decision-making processes.

1 **Decision-making power**: This dimension focuses on who makes decisions.

2 **Non-decision making**: This dimension of power examines who exercises power by limiting the range of alternatives to be considered. Some would argue that civil servants and council officials hold this type of power.

3 **Power to shape people's desires**: This dimension of power relates to who defines the terms within which debates take place. This requires an examination of the factors which influence decisions external to the process of decision making, e.g. in a community project funded by the local authority there is often a reluctance to protest against council policies because of a real or imagined risk that this will result in funding being withdrawn.

So far the theorists we have looked at in this section have concentrated on identifying who holds power and the kind of power they have. This is not very helpful when considering power relationships at an individual level and there is limited attention given to the ways in which people resist power and circumvent the power of decision making. This use of power is important in community and youth work because for the most part our work is with disenfranchised groups who do not feel that they have access to power.

Foucault (1979) is a key theorist who considers the way in which power operates in everyday life. He argues that there is a network of practices and institutions in society which effectively controls people and consequently governments do not need to assert their power in an explicit way. He points to the way in which surveillance, either by data collection or CCTV, individualises people and makes them observable. This leads to self-regulation. He also points to the way in which human sciences have led to the categorisation of people and enabled consideration of the extent to which people deviate from statistical norms. This is explored in more depth in Chapter 4.

This outline of the way in which social theorists consider power is fairly limited and you will need to read one of the text books listed at the end of the chapter to develop your understanding. My main concern is to encourage you to question power – who has it? How do they exert it? How can people gain power or recognise the power they have? Is the impact of power good or bad?

Power and class

In the section above we have identified that there are different explanations of how power operates in society. One of the ways in which these theories explore power has been in relation to stratification systems, i.e. how social groups are ranked in terms of prestige, wealth and power and why and how this is important in how societies operate. The aim of this section is to encourage you to think about how class operates as power based on your experience and then to evaluate this in the light of some theories.

We need first of all identify what social class is.

ACTIVITY 2.5

- *What social class are you and why?*

- *Compare your views with colleagues, family and friends. Do you agree on which class you belong to? Do you agree on the factors that determine your class?*

- *Does your class give you power or make it possible for others to oppress you?*

People often find it relatively easy to identify themselves with a particular social class but are less clear about the reasons. When I first started doing this exercise with groups of community and youth work students some 20 years ago the vast majority of students identified themselves as working class – mainly because they came from families where their father was employed in mining or shipbuilding as an unskilled or semi-skilled worker. Some suggested that they were working class because of their shared values. Today when I do this exercise considerably more students identify themselves as middle class, mainly because they either own or want to own their home or because they are studying at university, but there is also a sense that they don't want to be working class – they have aspirations and that means to them that they are not part of the working class. This begs the question about what has changed over the last 20 years. One way to answer this is to look at what social theorists have to say about class.

Until the 1980s the concept of social class, linking economic role, social identity and political affiliation was almost unanimously seen as central to sociological study, particularly in the UK.

There are three different but related ways in which social theorists understand class.

1 **Class as wealth**. Marx identified two basic classes – the bourgeoisie who own the means of production; and the proletariat who do not. Thus class is linked explicitly to wealth. Weber developed this view recognising that status gained from type of employment also gave individuals access to power.

2 **Class as occupation**. In Britain, for statistical purposes, class was defined using the Registrar General's scale of social class and socio-economic groups. This consisted of six major classes, ranging from 'Professionals' in class one to 'unskilled' and 'other' in classes 5 and 6. Class 3 was sub-divided into manual and non-manual skills. It has been argued that the level of skill at work may not be the best way of measuring access to social resources. The Registrar General's scale contained absurdities like equating small tenant farmers and major land owners. Some of these arguments have been addressed by the introduction of the National Statistics Socio-economic Classification (NS-SEC). This is based on the concepts of employment relations and conditions rather than skill.

3 **Class as values/belief systems/identity**. Usually based on a recognition of common interests.

During the last 25 years a number of writers, including Beck (1992), have questioned whether class still has relevance in a modern, pluralist welfare state. They have argued that class is not so important in defining who we are, how we behave or where our loyalties lie.

Yet there is considerable evidence that people in Britain still often identify themselves as members of a class and that significant correlations between class inequalities in health and life-chances continue to exist.

C H A P T E R   R E V I E W

This chapter has introduced a wide range of explanations about what society is and how it impacts on the practice of community and youth work. The chapter has demonstrated that the social world is complex and that theory can be helpful in providing a framework for making sense of our own thoughts.

We have highlighted theories which relate to society as a whole, those which relate to aspects of society such as communities and the way in which power is central to understanding the way in which society works. The theme of power is central to this book and it is taken up in all of the subsequent chapters in this book.

We have provided an overview of some of the key themes in social theory in order to help you understand a range of explanations about what the social world is and to begin to raise questions about how we know what the social world is. The key distinction is the different starting points of the theorists. Structural theorists start from the premise that society is depended on social systems and structures, for example the economic system, political system, religion, the family. Interpretive theorists start from the premise that society is dependent on the interactions of individuals. We have also highlighted that in order to understand society we need to consider whether individuals are self-seeking or altruistic – does society need to control individuals or provide opportunities for co-operation?

The exercises in the chapter have been designed to illustrate that whether we are conscious of it or not we all have 'theories' about society. It is also likely that our life experiences and our practice as community and youth workers has provided us with some evidence to support our 'theories'.

These texts are useful in understanding theories of community:

FURTHER READING

These general text books are useful to further your understanding of social theories:

Bilton, T with Bradbury, L, Stanyer, J and Stephens, P (2002) *Introductory sociology*. Basingstoke: Macmillan.

Crossley, N (2005) *Key concepts in critical social theory*. London: Sage.

Haralambos, M, Heald, RM and Holborn, M (2004) *Sociology themes and perspectives*. London: Collins. www.haralambosholborn.com/

These texts are useful in understanding theories of community:

Crow, G and Allan, G (1994) *Community life: an introduction to local social relations*. Hemel Hempstead: Harvester Wheatsheaf.

Putnam, RD (2000) *Bowling alone. the collapse and revival of American community*. New York: Simon and Schuster.

Worsley, P (1988) *The new introducing sociology*. Harmondsworth: Penguin. (Especially Chapter 7.)

This book provides information on completing a community profile:

Twelvetrees, A (2008) *Community work* (4th edition) Basingstoke: Palgrave Macmillan.

These texts are useful in understanding theories of power:

Bilton, T with Bradbury, L, Stanyer, J and Stephens, P (2002), *Introductory sociology*. Basingstoke: Macmillan.

Crossley, N (2005) *Key concepts in critical social theory*. London: Sage.

Haralambos, M, Heald, RM and Holborn, M (2004) *Sociology themes and perspectives*. London: Collins.

Lukes, S (1974) *Power: a radical view*. London: Macmillan.

USEFUL WEBSITES

www.haralambosholborn.com/

www.infed.org/

Chapter 3

Learning from lives

Rick Bowler
(with Ilona Buchroth and Chris Parkin)

CHAPTER OBJECTIVES

This chapter will help you meet the following National Occupational Standards.

1.1.1 Enable young people to use their learning to enhance their future development

1.3.1 Facilitate young people's exploration of their values and beliefs

2.3.3 Challenge oppressive behaviour in young people

3.1.2 Assist young people to express and to realise their goals

It will also introduce you to the following academic standards as set out in the youth and community work benchmark statement (2009, QAA).

7.1
• Recognise and compare multiple, competing perspectives and challenge the status quo and dominant perspectives.
• Question and be prepared to deconstruct taken for granted and common sense professional understandings.

7.2
• Identify discrimination, oppression and/or exclusion and be strategic in developing interventions to tackle these in different situations.

Introduction

This chapter will help you to learn from your own life experiences and to use theory to explore how values and beliefs have been developed. You will explore how reflecting on your own identity can assist you in understanding the lives of young people and adults that you work with as a professional worker. The chapter is concerned with the way people look at their lives, tell their stories and make sense of them within a wider social and political context. As workers in the social professions we become involved in people's lives in different ways and many of our interventions explicitly set out to have an impact on how people's lives unfold. The way we listen to others, and hear and interpret others' stories is intricately interwoven with the way we tell our own stories and how we explain the central features and aspects of our own development. How have we come to hold the views that we have?

What values are important to us? How have these come about? How do we interpret the stories and lives of others? What kind of view of the world guides our interpretation?

The chapter offers exercises and examples drawn from current policy and practice to identify practical ways in which we can use stories to better understand the importance of who we are, what we do and how we can contribute to transforming individual and collective lives.

There will be a specific focus on the extent to which our life experiences are influenced by dominant systems of power and knowledge to help us to understand how to challenge unequal power structures.

It is important to recognise that our experiences, the ways we express them and the meanings we derive from them are not an objective account of facts. They happen in a political context where social and cultural practices are produced and reproduced. While exploring individual life stories we also need to consider the 'social world' people inhabit and distinguish between what could be termed biographical 'facts' and which elements are socially constructed. In this context we are looking at what people choose to tell, how they interpret the world they inhabit and how power relationships shape lives and the resulting stories.

The first section will consider why it is important to learn from lives in professional practice. It will help you to be clear about the ways in which life stories relate to the purpose of community and youth work practice. It will begin by examining theory which relates to the value and purpose of learning from lives before exploring in more detail a range of theory which will help you to learn from your own and other people's life stories.

The next section will draw on a range of theories which relate to the development of identity and ways of learning from life stories. A key aim of this chapter is to help you develop a critical perspective and understand the impact of dominant ways of thinking and acting on our experiences. Activities which encourage you to reflect on your own lives by applying some of the theories introduced will be a particular aspect of this chapter.

The final section will consider the use of life stories in practice examining practical ways of telling and hearing stories and linking those to the professional interventions that are designed to challenge discrimination.

Why work with life stories

For community and youth workers, and other related professionals, there are a number of reasons why it is useful to learn from our own and other people's life stories.

A systematic way of learning from experience

We know that a good start to understanding theory is to critically interrogate our own lives and the ways in which our experiences have impacted on our personality, life chances and belief systems. Comparing our experiences with others also helps us to recognise the way in which similar experiences may affect us differently. We have already seen in Chapter 1 how theory can be developed by using our experiences but we have also begun to consider the shortfalls of relying solely on these experiences; nevertheless it is always useful to reflect on how our own experiences relate to theory – you should find that you can reflect on all the theory introduced in this book in relation to your own experiences.

In particular because our lives are influenced by the social, political and cultural context, reflecting on life stories can help us to understand how theory relates to real lived experiences. This can help us to understand why and how theory relates to practice. Using life stories or biographies is an accepted method of developing theory. One extensive example is Henderson et al. (2007) who used a biographical approach to exploring young people's perspectives on growing up at the turn of the twenty-first century.

A way of understanding identity

What makes us the people we are, and what links us to other people is closely connected with the concept of 'identity'. Our identity can be how we see ourselves and also how others see us. It is therefore both personal and social. The personal describes the inner world, our view of self, our thoughts, values and feelings and our sense of agency. The social is relational and encompasses beliefs, interests, cultural expectations, our place in the world and our ways of being with others in it. Moreover, many aspects of our identity are socially significant, as they play powerful roles in securing privileges or embedding disadvantage.

A way of considering the purpose and process of assessment frameworks

Current government policy requires a collaborative approach to meeting the needs of children and young people. This is achieved by assessment using a common framework with the young person themselves being a key player in both the assessment of need and identification of appropriate responses (DCFS, Targeted Youth Support, 2009). In order to assess, questions have to be asked and stories told. An understanding of the way in which identities are formed, the impact of social, cultural and political contexts and an appreciation of power relationships are key to this process.

A way of recognising the impact of oppression and discrimination to help us identify interventions which will challenge power and inequality

Identity is influenced by a complex interplay of processes determined by power relationships within society as a whole. The ways we know the world and the ways we practice in it are inextricably linked. Understanding the impact of power and inequality in our own lives will help us to recognise and respond to the issues facing the wide range of people we encounter in practice. It has also been suggested that the way in which we tell and share stories can transcend barriers, challenge unjust authority and facilitate individual and collective change opening up new and better ways of knowing and living (Wiessner, 2005).

Now we have established a number of good reasons why we as professional workers are concerned with life stories, we need to look in more detail at the various issues that arise out of our engagement with people, their experiences and their stories. We need to set the scene.

ACTIVITY 3.1

Think about any moments in your life where you have engaged in a dialogue with a professional agency and worker. This could be when you needed or met the doctor, the dentist, a police officer, civil servant, the school, the college/university or the local authority. Walk yourself through the journey and identify the occasions when you were engaged with and spoken to.

- *Can you identify moments when you experienced comfort or discomfort on that journey? Make notes on what was said, how the other person behaved, what they did.*

- *Did the other person's language, behaviour, knowledge impact on what happened next? Was what happened next safer and less anxious for you or less safe and more anxiety provoking? Were their stories different to yours?*

- *If the experience was positive what happened to make you feel an equal participant?*

- *If the experience was uncomfortable, in what ways did the professional power make you experience a sense of being disempowered?*

- *Can you tell whether your story was listened to?*

Reflecting on your experiences is likely to have brought out a number of the key elements that help people be in tune with themselves, their stories and their sense of agency. Moreover, it indicates important aspects of our professional roles and the need to carefully look at issues of power and the act of listening and understanding within the context of inherently unequal relationships.

How life stories are constructed

Looking at the way life stories are constructed provides a number of important indicators for the way people make sense of their lives. Reflecting on the process of inviting people to talk about their lives is linked to many issues that also arise in life history and biographical research.

To start off, it is important to remember that life stories are not an objective 'account of facts', although this may be hidden in the way conversations about lives are encouraged to unfold. Bourdieu refers to dominant conversational patterns as a 'biographical illusion' that treats life as a coherent story based on a chronological sequence of meaningful events. We need to allow for the possibility therefore that the structures of life stories reflect the way we invite people to talk about them rather than it being a true indication of how people actually make sense of their lives. Furthermore, it may well be that the structure of a conversation encourages a relationship of causality or chronology that might not be chosen by participants themselves as *in accounting for a life . . . the little snippets of narrative told in an interview are sewn together to generate a different kind of unity from any that may be perceived by the teller* (Schostak, 2006, p141).

Bruner (2004) suggests that there are structural similarities between the 'self' and the chosen narrative – for example, those with a clearer sense of self also tell stories with a more distinct purpose, that is they portray their lives in a more orderly and purposeful manner. This could also mean that they might be more selective in the telling and more mindful of the impression they make on the listener. For Bruner this reflects considerations of the private and the public, as no narrative can exist very well without consideration of what the listener will think. This has important implications as the context as well as the presumed or expressed expectations of the listener will shape the telling of a life story in particular ways. As the structure of the conversation itself may encourage a particular sequence of events, societal expectations encourage or discourage particular aspects and thus the telling of the story is embedded in the traditions of what social norms allow participants to share. For example, when students are asked about their motivation to go to university they will often talk about career aspirations as the dominant discourse tends to link educational experiences to instrumental outcomes. However, for many students, particularly non-standard entrants to higher education, the less articulated, 'unofficial' motivation may well lie somewhere entirely different and relate more closely to the need to fulfil ambitions that have been denied in the past. In a similar way the comments a young person may make on social networking sites about their experiences of education may be very different to the way they would talk about their lives on a face to face basis with their tutors or family.

ACTIVITY **3.2**

Think of a period of your life and imagine talking about it in different circumstances. For example, which aspect of this section of your life would you tell a close friend, your parents, a career adviser, during a job interview, to a therapist, at a party?

It is quite likely that you will have chosen very different aspects of your story in each scenario, but also that you probably would have felt comfortable being asked to tell the story in some situations and less so in others. It is also possible, depending on your own cultural background, the social and cultural capital you carry and your own sense of agency, that you might have known intuitively what was acceptable and required of you. Knowing the rules of engagement and whether you are an 'insider' or 'outsider' are crucial components in what is being shared.

By engaging in narratives people start to make sense of their lives. The process of telling requires people to order their experiences in some coherent way and make sense of what the 'ingredients' of that story should be.

For the next few sections we suggest that you use your own life story as a case study. This may take you some time and you will find your own way of making sense of the various influences that have shaped your development. To start with, think of the way you might want to structure your own story – what could be the possible headings you are going to use?

What did this exercise encourage you to think about? How did you structure your story? Did you primarily concentrate on dates and events or did you also start to think about influences of others, thoughts and feelings that accompanied your life story? Let us explore a little more what some of the typical elements of a life story could be.

Significant life events/fateful moments

Many people structure their life stories around periods of transition or some of the key milestones in their lives. These could include starting school, moving house, the birth of a sibling, leaving home or getting a job. A further structure of a life story sometimes evolves out of looking at events and key moments that in some way changed your life in a significant way. Denzin (1989, p22) claims that the idea that lives are turned around by significant live events is firmly established in Western thought and narratives are therefore typically structured around these events that he refers to as 'epiphanies'. Similar sentiments are expressed by Giddens who talks about *fateful moments . . . when individuals are called on to take decisions that are particularly consequential for their ambitions, or more generally for their future lives* (Giddens, 1991, p112). Other people can recall crises in their lives that required them to re-evaluate and re-think previous patterns of behaviour. Many people are confronted with experiences, and at times dilemmas, that severely test assumed truths and prompt people to critically reflect on values, assumptions and beliefs and re-assess their validity. Returning to the life story you recorded earlier, did you recall critical moments or key events that structured your account of your life events? Can you think of examples that you feel changed your path in life in some way? What would your life story look like now if you were concentrating on these 'fateful moments'?

Key people

A further aspect of reflections on lives usually refers to key people and relationships. Who were the people who made an impact on you and shaped your life? Were they inside or outside the family? What was it that made them so important in your life? Was their impact a hindrance or an encouragement? Have you learned important things from them?

The impact that key people can have in motivating and mobilising others is well documented in a range of studies, in particular with reference to pathways to learning and volunteering – people are much more likely to get involved in new things if somebody asks them to.

Values

When you were thinking about your life story did you consider how you came to hold the views that are important to you? How have these views been shaped? How would you describe your values?

Have these been influenced by significant life events or have they been 'taught' to you by influential people? Are there family traditions or religious affiliations that have shaped your understanding of what you consider to be 'right or wrong'? In what way do you think the values you hold are bound up with the way you see yourself and describe yourself? In what way do you think your values have influenced choices that you have made in your life – for example, to embark on this particular course of study? You might want to look at the relationship between your personal values and the professional values expressed by your professional body – do you see particular relationships?

How we hear stories

In addition to being 'story tellers' we are often at the receiving ends of other people's stories and their attempts to understand and reflect on how their life events have influenced and shaped them. Looking at our own ways of approaching life stories has given us some vital clues to how the process works, but we need to look more specifically now at our own roles as being listeners to the stories of others. Although as practitioners we often talk about being neutral and unbiased, we need to explore the reality of this in more detail. Here we can learn something from theories on qualitative research methods using interviews as a form of data collection. The concept of 'reflexivity' is important here, for instance the process by which we acknowledge the way the research process and the researcher shape the outcome. Our own identities as listeners of stories matter greatly. For example, our beliefs, politics, values, gender and race will impact on how we establish rapport, what kinds of questions we ask, how the answers are 'heard' and how we make sense of what we hear. The stories we hear are therefore not a representation of 'facts', but the result of a relational process that generates 'situated knowledge'. Feminist writers in particular question claims of 'objectivity' in research in the way it is often presented in positivist research paradigms, and Harding (1991) therefore differentiates between 'weak' and 'strong' objectivity or 'reflexivity'. She suggests that 'strong' objectivity/reflexivity is achieved by researchers laying open the way their background and value base has shaped the research process rather than creating an illusion of detachment.

Please imagine yourself as a professional in the following case study.

CASE STUDY

Teenage pregnancy

Claire is a 16-year-old woman who has been coming to your youth club for a number of years. She had been a regular attender when she was younger, but less so over the past year. Claire is now pregnant by her partner who is significantly older than her and who is often not around for long periods of time. Claire is unwilling to tell you more about him or the reasons for his absence. She has been living with her mum until now but is planning to get a flat for herself when the baby is born. Her mum will not be able to support her financially. Clare has a fairly stable group of friends, some from school and others from the youth club who she spends a lot of her time with.

Claire has not finished her GCSEs, because she feels uncomfortable being at school now, but she says she might go to college later.

What kinds of issues did this case study raise for you? What do you think are the most urgent issues to address with Claire? Do these issues change from the perspective of different professionals?

What are your views about young parents? What is your 'hunch' about Claire's partner? What do you think about her plans for living independently or her views on her education?

The processes you are involved in here are closely aligned to the methods of reflection that we deal with in more detail in Chapter 6. The act of listening is a dynamic and active process that requires you to both be vigilant when you are listening and mindful of the interventions you are choosing. These forms of reflection require you to be involved in a constant checking of your own position and perspective. As mentioned above, as the listener to a story you are in a similar position to that of a researcher. Rather than maintaining the illusion of detachment referred to above you are aiming for the strong reflexivity that requires a careful appraisal of what you bring to the process. The 'I have been there myself' realisation for example can sometimes provide a powerful starting point to establish rapport, but also has serious limitations. Your own experience of a similar scenario may well get in the way of you listening carefully to the other person without overlaying their experience with yours. Conversely – you might be out of your depth and understanding can only be achieved by acknowledging your limitations and through a willingness to let go of the 'taken for granted' or previously established routines.

These processes of reflection also require you to be clear about the relationship between rapport and neutrality. Rapport requires you to establish a relationship with the person you are in a conversation with while still maintaining a neutral position to what is being said to you. Maria Mies describes this form of involvement as 'conscious partiality' which she regards as being in direct opposition to the impartial, 'spectator-knowledge' that is acquired by a disinterested and distant relationship to the research 'subject' (Mies, 1993, p68). For Mies this conscious partiality puts both the participant and the researcher into a larger social context.

If you now return to your thoughts about Claire in the case study, think about how you as a person might impact on your relationship and in particular your rapport with her. For example you might want think about questions like these.

- Which aspects of yourself make you a particularly useful person to work with Claire?

- What do you think the barriers might be in your working relationship with her?

- How do the values you hold influence the way you will work with Claire?

- What assumptions have you made about Claire's race, social class, religious affiliations? How might these influence the way you will work with her?

- Do you think your own gender, race, social class, educational background make a difference to maintaining a rapport with Claire?

The context of telling and hearing stories

In the last section we explored the reflexivity of telling and hearing stories from a primarily individual perspective. However, a further important aspect of learning from life stories is to situate them in their historical, social, cultural and political contexts, and we will be looking more specifically at issues of power and inequality and how these shape the way we tell and hear life stories. As we saw in Chapter 1, listening to stories and the way in which we interpret them depends on an understanding of the factors or 'theory' which influences the story. In Activity 2.1 we explored how the way in which we tell our stories is influenced by how we think they will be interpreted. Other chapters in this book will help you to understand various aspects of the context for our stories – for example the social and educational context.

The following section will focus on relating the context of our stories to the way in which we describe ourselves.

How are we described and how do we describe ourselves

Language

Life story telling and biographical work rely on the medium of language. However, language itself is not neutral, but can be used to the benefit or detriment of different groups of people. Dale Spender in her book *Man made language* (1980) challenges the myth of neutrality and indicates how language is used to both reflect and maintain unequal power relationships. Any language, developing and changing over time, will usually reflect the status quo within a society. Words that are used to describe particular groups or their actions will therefore generally reflect the value, status and positioning that this group or that action occupies within society. One common method is the gendered process of naming similar actions. She identifies how different words are used to describe the same actions performed by women or men. The words that are used for example to describe women's talk often have a negative connotation or devalue the activity (gossip, jabber, prattle, gab) whereas men engage in much more serious encounters as they discuss and debate.

ACTIVITY **3.4**

Take a particular group you regularly come across in your professional life – for example, young people, people who belong to a majority group, people who belong to a minority group, young parents. Over the course of a week, try to list the positive and negative words and descriptions you come across. Is one list longer than the other?

You have probably found that it is easier to find comments about the minority groups and these are likely to be more negative than positive descriptions. The majority group is often everywhere and nowhere in public commentary. It is not uncommon that marginalised and less powerful groups find it difficult to feel represented or at home in the dominant public language that is available. Here we can see the impact language can have in maintaining inequality as it is difficult to correct a negative description if the language has no words to do this with. Black people and women, for example, have fought long and hard to challenge norms within the English language that renders them invisible or inferior. These gendered and racialised ways of narrating and ordering the world, when exposed, are often met with resistance because the dominant culture has defined language as neutral and objective. Dominant groups in society often attempt to defend the use of language that is discriminatory to others on the grounds of a presumed neutrality of language and meaning. We can begin to understand that what is regarded as objectivity is often the accepted subjectivity of the more powerful.

ACTIVITY **3.5**

Try to solve the following conundrum

A man meets an old friend who, since their last meeting, has married and has a young child. The man looks at his friend's child and exclaims 'My dear, you look just like your mother!' How does the man know this?

For those of you who took a little time to work out the answer – if the term 'friend' was indeed gender neutral, as English grammar says it is, you would have realised immediately that the friend was the mother of the child. For a lot of people the term 'friend' conjures up a male image especially when, as in the example above, we are talking about the friend of a man. The issue here is that what might be regarded as correct and the norm in the language does not always match what is understood and associated with it. Because the language we use is socially constructed it can serve as a powerful tool to maintain and entrench unequal power relationships as well as impose unwanted identities.

A further challenge to the presumed neutrality of the language we use lies in the way it indicates what is considered to be the norm and what is the deviation from the norm. This means that the world is viewed and described from the perspective of dominant groups. Take for example the use of the BME (black and minority ethnic) category which has become a standard descriptor of a minority status in Britain. This has more recently been changed to BAME (black Asian minority ethnic). This reflects a status that is positioned in contrast to a white majority norm.

Identity

What makes us the people we are, what links us to other people and how self is linked to other are closely connected with the concept of 'identity'. Our identity can be how we see ourselves and also how others see us. It is therefore both personal and social. The personal describes the inner world, our view of self, our thoughts, values and feelings and our sense of agency. The social is relational and encompasses beliefs, interests, cultural expectations, our place in the world and our ways of being with others in it. How this identity is arrived at is a complex interplay of processes determined by power relationships within society as a whole.

As a starting point it is useful to look at the way people's personal and social identities are shaped by the way people are grouped and described. Loosely based on 'labelling' theory, let us explore the labels that are attached to groups of people and how these define their position in life (Becker, 1963). Labelling theory makes an important distinction between the actions that people engage in and the labels that are attached to them as a result. In these ideas it is the label more than the action that leads to the meanings given to somebody's identity. There is therefore a difference between people who have been assigned a label and those who engage in the same activity but are not labelled in the same way.

Children for example may take things from other children when they are young but will not necessarily be 'labelled' or develop into 'thieves'. Similarly, some young people engage in activities that are not strictly lawful but will not ultimately acquire the label of 'criminal'. Here we can see that the label 'criminal' and 'thief' carry meanings that are dependent on context and particular knowledge systems. In their work on 'Policing the Crisis' Hall et al. (1978) identified that the 'labels' mugger and mugging were politicised and racialised. Black young men, irrespective of evidence, context, social conditions, the legacy and daily experiences of state, cultural and personal racism, or of the similarities between all young people when 'hanging about', were constructed in the popular imagination as aggressive, violent and criminal. Deviance for example is therefore not based on the behaviour of people, but reflects the ability of the powerful to label the behaviour of others. Norms, and accordingly deviance, can change with time and are often applied unequally to different groups of people. Labels therefore can become closely linked to a person's identity and affect the way they see themselves and are seen by others.

ACTIVITY **3.6**

What kinds of 'labels' can you think of that would describe yourself? Try to think of as many as possible. Mind map them:

- *How have these labels come about?*

- *Which ones have you chosen yourself? Which ones have been assigned to you by others (maybe professionals)?*

- *Which labels are helpful to you, which ones are a hindrance?*

Doing this exercise you are quite likely to have identified some labels that you are proud of and some that you might have been given by others that you might not agree with or think were never justified. Labels (categories) have the potential to shape the person's opportunities and life chances in quite significant ways.

First, these labels can become internalised and have a self-regulatory or a restrictive function in that people can start believing what the label suggests about themselves. These processes of internalisation can, and do, de-power people and restrict their agency. They colonise the mind in much the same way that colonial powers colonised the mindsets of whole communities and societies. Moreover, as we see in more detail in Chapter 4, internalising restrictive labels plays an important role in sanctioning and legitimising unequal power relationships. For example many students from working class backgrounds, men, women, black and white, enter further and higher education with a degree of personal and social trepidation. They may have not been taught, nor rehearsed, all the rules for playing the game. These students then, rather than looking at a particular incident – for example, 'I have not done very well in this assignment' – see this as confirmation of the label 'I am not/I never have been very academic'. This label of 'not very academic' carries attributes that can suggest 'not clever, never going to be clever enough' and even 'not university material'. These internalised, and often unconscious acceptances of negative attributes, get in the way of accurately solving the right problem. It will affect attempting particular tasks or impact upon the choices that people make in their lives.

Second, at the social level labels can become the key to opening and closing, revealing or hiding doors and confer privilege or disadvantage.

Labels can become an important part of what a person will regard or be assigned as their identity. Looking at the labels you have given yourself in Activity 3.6, you will probably find a few that are of a descriptive nature and others that can be called socially significant. The former may only serve to describe a particular aspect of yourself – for instance you are a 'red head', a 'book lover', a 'stamp collector'. Socially significant categories on the other hand, such as being working class, black or female, matter in terms of how they position you within society. However, there are (of course) a number of categories, especially within youth culture that are shifting from a descriptive to a socially significant label, as people identify and are placed increasingly according to their tastes and consumer behaviour.

Other identities that you may have identified in the last activity may be linked to the beliefs you hold. In addition to being potentially socially significant these identities linked to beliefs can also mean that people can become quite fixed in their thinking, as a challenge to their belief system can also pose a threat to their identity.

A further outcome of your reflections on labels and identities could have revealed a range of different identities that co-exist and come to the forefront at different times and on different occasions. As a result, multiple identities will also allow people to construct different and parallel narratives of their lives. Whether these identities are of equal status or are pulled together under a more prominent heading that reflects an overarching identity or 'self' is still a question of academic debate – what do you think?

Collective identities
Labels and their resulting identities go beyond the positioning of individuals but also play a crucial part in the way different groups in society see themselves and each other. Looking at collective identities from a critical perspective demands we ask who has been involved in shaping the collective identity and who is likely to gain from it. We draw on the work of Michel Foucault and discuss in more detail in Chapters 1 and 4 how people are often

grouped around the potential issues they pose for society with the view of making them visible and ultimately more controllable. The collective identities and labels arising from this process usually have two important features: they are not generally chosen by the people thus described and therefore are not meaningful categories to them; and the collective labels help reinforce dominant societal norms and have the capacity to render people 'outsiders'. 'Single parents', 'teenage mothers', 'NEETs', 'asylum seekers' are not descriptive labels, but they position people on society's margin and focus on their potential issues or deficits.

Labels and social categories are therefore not neutral, natural or objective descriptions of groups of people, they can change and acquire different meanings over time – they are, as we stated earlier, socially constructed and are therefore open to deconstruction and reconstruction. Reconstruction is important because, as Parekh points out, collective identities can also be developed with a powerful, liberating dimension (Parekh, 2008). People form alliances often directly in response to a negative identity they have been assigned. They 'voice' their experiences and tell alternative stories that challenge unjust cultures and structures in society. They could be seeking 'liberation' from unjust systems or 'pride' in a previously negatively given label or activity. In Britain the trade unions, the women's liberation movement, gay pride, the black power and Asian youth movements and the disability rights movement are all forms of 'oppressed' collectives that have organised for social justice collaboratively around and across their group identities.

Forging alliances and supporting alternative collective identities is a prominent concern of community and youth workers' role of with working with people on their shared concerns and issues. However, we need to also refer to the point raised by Crossley (2005) that of course all collective identities are relational – in order for somebody to belong somebody needs to 'un-belong'. Collective identities arguably all depend on some form of internal coherence that defines their membership, which in turn has the capacity to (re)produce 'insider' and 'outsider' relationships.

ACTIVITY **3.7**

Think about the place (s) you were born into and grew up in.

Birth   3   6   9   12   16

You could mark the points when you moved between birth and 16 years old. Some people never move during their upbringing, others move regularly and others have to move for reasons entirely outside of their own and their family's/carers' control.

Pick one particular place and time when you were settled the longest.

- *Did you feel that you were at 'home' during that period?*

- *Did you feel and think you were part of the majority or minority culture in the local area you were living in?*

ACTIVITY **3.7** *continued*

- *In a very general sense, these thoughts and feelings relate to whether you hold some aspects of insider or outsider knowledge. Was gender, 'race', faith, sexuality, class or disability a part of the feelings and thoughts about being an insider or outsider? What stories would you tell about these moments?*

- *Make some notes on what memories you have about what you experienced, felt and thought, about being an insider. Did you ever know 'outsiders'? What did you know about them?*

- *For those whose experience, at that time, was as an outsider, make some notes on how you knew you were not an insider.*

Engaging in these reflections is likely to have highlighted the rich and varied issues that the term 'belonging' can be associated with. For some people belonging is linked to a particular aspect of geography, others link it to religious beliefs, others again think of political affiliations, race, sexuality or gender. Of course it also possible that a prevailing sense of 'un-belonging' has shaped your identity. Your reflections are also likely to have started you thinking about some of the processes that are involved in creating insider and outsider positions; it is these processes that we will examine more closely in the following sections.

Stories from the edge

Telling and hearing stories does not operate on a level playing field. Some stories are heard and others kept hidden, 'silenced' and distant from our senses and experiences. Stories, as we can begin to discern, are not neutral. The voices we hear, the identities we see, and the voices and identities we are given access to are not neutral processes. Many people's realities are far removed from societal norms and the interpretative and communicative devices of dominant cultures do not make space for alternative realities. The resulting silencing of the 'unofficial' stories in turn helps to consolidate dominant norms. This can work essentially in two different ways:

- some stories are told but not heard;

- some stories are not being told.

Let us see how this works in practice. Marginalised groups are generally represented by those that are more powerful – so their voice and agency is restricted. Furthermore their experience is refracted through the lens of a dominant discourse that assigns them their status and quality.

ACTIVITY **3.8**

Look at a group of marginalised people that you are currently working with or indeed you belong to yourself. Over the period of a week try to collect the official stories that you can find for example in the press, through current government policy, the media in general.

ACTIVITY **3.8** *continued*

- *How does the official depiction and description compare to your insider knowledge?*

- *Which aspects of your experience are adequately represented, which aspects are not?*

- *What difference do you think it would make if the true stories were known?*

What did your research reveal? It is quite likely that you found significant discrepancies between the stories that people tell about themselves and others tell about them. Take the example of teenage parents; it is very common that teenage parents are portrayed from the angle of the potential societal issues they pose. As a result the overriding image is one of deficiency rather than strength. However, stories from young parents themselves can reveal a very different picture that is characterised by joy and resilience, elaborate coping mechanisms, and real determination to provide the best for their children – indeed, the stories you would find from parents of any age.

A further example in this context is the dominance of the portrayal of asylum seekers who we are told are 'flooding' the country and are portrayed as a source of problems for the 'host' community. These stories have the capacity to 'drown' out the 'voices from the margins' that speak alternative 'truths' about the human experiences of hope and contribution that are at the heart and in the spirit of the global refugee community.

As we explored in more detail in Chapter 1, in terms of who contributes to the development of theory, we see that marginalised groups do not have access to the channels of communication that would enable them to communicate a different perspective on their reality. The question of 'voice' is a therefore a recurring theme for community and youth workers and requires a focus on methods of engagement and meaningful participation. However, the issue of alternative realities goes beyond a pure acceptance that there might be another 'side of the story'. Patricia Hill Collins (2000), using black women's experience as an example, outlines the way in which unequal power relationships shape all aspects of knowledge and its generation (epistemology), as it is the dominant culture that determines what is worth investigating, which methods are going to be used, how the results are being interpreted, which tests it needs to withstand and how the knowledge is going to be used and ultimately who is going to be believed. As a result all other knowledge that is not 'validated' as such becomes 'subjugated' knowledge. As the means of disseminating and sharing knowledge, especially through the written word, are also regulated within the same dominant paradigm the importance of stories and the use of narratives becomes particularly important.

> *Telling stories is traditional in many cultures. In the oral tradition the African griot or storyteller passes on tales from generation to generation. In India the Hindu Ramayana, with its miracle plays and parables, tells epic stories of the battle between the gods for good and evil. In the academic world we use critical race theory, which is based on situational and reflexive knowledge, to illuminate hidden or marginal social realities. Stories are a powerful way to talk.*

(Mirza, 2008, p1)

A further layer of subjugated knowledge arises from the possibility that some stories are not told at all. Some dominant societal concepts and norms can acquire a near mythical status and their validity is not questioned in a public domain. People whose actual experiences do not conform to these norms are therefore more likely to regard themselves as deficient rather than criticise the inappropriate norm. Ann Oakley (2005) outlines how motherhood for example, rather than being authenticated by the actual experience of women, is held in tension between the extremes of male medical control of childbirth and an idealised, romantic perspective of mothering. The latter in particular poses a problem for articulating experiences that fall outside the prescriptive norm, without attracting labels of being 'abnormal'. The lack of articulation then has a self-regulatory function and helps to maintain an unrealistic standard. Consciousness raising groups and the claim of the feminist movement that the 'personal is political' laid some of the foundations of work that encourages people to share their real experience and foster solidarity with others to provide a counter reality. This contrast between actual, lived experience and dominant, normative portrayal of reality has acquired a further, contemporary dimension. People's lives have become more public as more intimate details are shared through a much wider range of media. Reality TV shows, self help books, social networking sites are now likely to reveal personal information and discuss issues that would have previously remained in a private sphere. However, this also means that media acquire a normative function for governing private lives to a greater extent and therefore an important role in perpetuating dominant ideas. As a result there is now a growing academic interest focusing on the roles of professionals to analyse how media construct meaning, create values and to develop a different form of critical media literacy (Kellner, 1995) that focuses on media discourses and representations.

Reconstructions

Not only do our own stories differ depending on the context we are telling them in, our perspectives on our own life change with time; as Goodson and Sikes point out, *life is a processual matter rather than a product* (Goodson and Sikes, 2001, p42). We are therefore reminded that a 'life' is always the past as it is reconstructed by the participant in the present and even more importantly with the knowledge and understanding of the present.

As people develop they also draw on different conceptual tools to interpret the aspects of their own lives or attach a different significance to events. So in some ways the process of 'story telling' appears to be happening on two separate levels for some people, as they follow a chronological pattern, attempting to recall what they saw as 'facts', but also offering different interpretations of cause and effect. Experiences and the interpretation of experiences are therefore intertwined (Lawler, 2002) and can change with each telling.

Fostering an ability to reflect on life in different ways is closely linked to the broadly educational processes that we are part of as professional workers. These include processes of deconstruction and challenging some of the deeply embedded ideas that people have developed over time. Many of these process are closely linked to asking different questions and critically examining many of the underlying assumptions that govern our lives (also see the section on hegemony in Chapter 4). Taking the example of a person talking about their educational experiences, they may initially come up with a statement like 'I was hopeless at school'. This particular statement may well have significant implications for the choices that this person would make about further study or careers, including a level of confidence relating to a range of tasks that might require certain skills. At a different period in their life this person, with the help of say theoretical and political perspectives, may reflect on their school life quite differently and for example look on their lack of achievement as a working class child in a predominantly middle class school. They might draw on an understanding of gender and race to identify how inequalities in the education system put them at a disadvantage. Although the net result – a lack of educational achievement – might be the same, the way the person's identity is constructed and the resulting ambitions for the future can then be dramatically different. Moreover, part of the reconstruction process allows people to put personal experiences into a wider societal and political context. As we have seen above, when we were talking about collective identities and untold stories, developing a collective perspective and voice plays a crucial part in challenging inequality and marginalisation. Community and youth workers play important roles here; as we outline in Chapter 4 learning to challenge the 'taken for granted' is a pivotal aspect of an emancipatory curriculum through which people's events are reinterpreted and life stories can be retold in different versions. As Steph Lawler points out *narrative . . . both connotes and constitutes movement – the movement from the potential to the actual, from what could be to what is, from past to present, from present to future* (2002, p250).

C H A P T E R R E V I E W

This chapter outlined the significance and importance of people's stories and the importance narratives have in professional practice. The way we listen to others, hear and interpret other stories is intricately interwoven with the way we tell and know our own. How we know who we are will directly impact on how and what we hear other people tell us. We were also reminded that narratives have an important role to play in generating alternative forms of knowledge that might otherwise not be possible to emerge within dominant structures that shape what is considered to be 'normal' and 'acceptable'.

To pay due regard to the importance of life stories, we need to understand something about the contexts in which lives and their resulting stories are told and developed. As practitioners we therefore engage in a very particular form of active listening that reflects our under-standing of power relationships, and of oppression in the widest possible sense, such as racism and sexism, issues of social class, disability or sexuality, as well as our knowledge of the realties and circumstances of people's lives. This active listening process also requires us to look at the language that is used to tell stories, for instance how people talk about themselves and others. Listening to stories and creating opportunities for alternative realities to be heard is a political act in its own right. As professionals we then need to think about the forms of intervention that follow our understanding of others and our insight into the stories from the margins. As we have seen in this chapter, and will explore further in the remaining chapters of this book, critical understanding informs the way we question dominant perspectives and support others to organise around common issues. This is by its very nature a collective concern.

FURTHER READING

Henderson S, Holland, J, McGrellis S, Sharpe S, Thomson R (2007) *Inventing adulthoods: a biographical approach to youth transitions*. London: Sage.

Excellent biographical approach to understanding the complexities of contemporary young people's lives in Britain.

Lawler, S (2002) 'Narrative in social research' in May, T (ed) *Qualitative research in action*. London: Sage.

Very good and detailed reflections on how narratives relate to people's socially located lives and identities.

Parekh, B (2008) *A new politics of identity: political principles for an interdependent world*. Basingstoke: Palgrave Macmillan.

Detailed exploration of different aspects of identity.

Kehily, MJ (ed) (2007) *Understanding youth: Perspectives, identities and practices*. London: Sage.

Extensive overview of young people's perspectives on identity.

Harding, S (1991) *Whose science? Whose knowledge? Thinking from women's lives*. Ithaca, NY: Cornell University Press.

Chapter 4
Education

Ilona Buchroth

CHAPTER OBJECTIVES

This chapter will help you meet the following National Occupational Standards.

1.1.1 Enable young people to use their learning to enhance their future development

1.4.1 Provide information and support to young people

1.4.2 Enable young people to access information and to make decisions

2.3.2 Develop a culture and systems that promote equality and value diversity

5.3.2 Provide learning opportunities for colleagues

It will also introduce you to the following academic standards as set out in the youth and community work benchmark statement (2009, QAA).

7.1
- Recognise and compare multiple, competing perspectives and challenge the status quo and dominant perspectives.
- Facilitate informal learning and community development using group work and a range of interpersonal skills.
- Question and be prepared to deconstruct taken for granted and common sense professional understandings.

7.2
- Identify discrimination, oppression and/or exclusion and be strategic in developing interventions to tackle these in different situations.

Introduction

The relationship between community and youth work and education is wide-reaching and multi-faceted.

First, the most obvious link is to informal education, which underlies many of the community and youth work's central themes of empowerment, social justice, democracy and liberation. As such community and youth work is inherently always an educational activity, based on dialogue and conversation, working with the issues that people bring from their everyday lives. Much of this form of education is outside mainstream or traditional educational settings and community and youth workers enter into a voluntary relationship, facilitating or setting the scene for learning that involves all participants on an equal basis.

Second, people's experiences of education and their resulting attitude to learning is often a central element of the issues that community and youth workers deal with. The effects of formal education and schooling, in the way these affect people's life chances, their perception of themselves and others, often leave a lasting legacy. As a result, much of what community and youth workers encounter, either directly, or indirectly, relates to what people feel they are capable of, what can be changed and how much influence they have over the conditions that shape their lives. This inevitably requires us to think about equality and inequality, the distribution of power and (dis)advantage and the role that learning and education plays in this context.

And third, community and youth workers enter into a relationship with other forms of education as we work with and in schools, or enter into contracts to deliver particular forms of remedial educational measures. Similarly community and youth workers work with other, related professions in shared educational projects, such as health promotion, youth justice or early years' professionals. Many of the professional relationships we enter into therefore require us to negotiate our educational positions and approaches. In this process we have to be clear to ourselves and others about the central features of our educational work.

This chapter looks at education in the wider sense. It explores some of the underlying concepts that make up and shape educational experiences, how learning is influenced by a range of different forces within society and how these interact with and are shaped by power. An exploration of education and power will therefore take us into the area of 'critical' theory (which we discussed further in Chapter 2), and we will explore concepts such as 'hegemony', 'capital' and the roles of 'intellectuals'.

There are many different definitions and approaches to explaining how different power relationships come about and you might find it useful to explore some sociological texts for definitions. Generally speaking, looking at power can either take us into a discussion of *who* has power over whom or *how* the processes work that keep power relationships in place. For this chapter we will mainly be concentrating on the latter; for instance we will be looking at:

- how education can create and maintain power imbalances;

- how education can work towards redressing some of these power imbalances and develop a transformative approach.

What is a curriculum?

In this chapter we will examine different versions of what constitutes a curriculum. For example, trying to answer questions such as the following will take us into a discussion of what constitutes a curriculum in the broadest sense.

- What do we learn at home and what at school?

- Why is being good at skate boarding less well thought of than being able to play the piano?

- Why can you learn about fixing a car but not about stealing one?

- Why are adult education classes funded for literacy, but not for nail art?

This means not just looking at formal education, but exploring more generally what is learned by whom, how access to education is regulated, what the methods and purposes of learning are, how learning is evaluated and which different roles learners, teachers and professionals can take in this process.

ACTIVITY 4.1

Design a curriculum. First, choose an area of interest – maybe drug education for young people or healthy eating for pensioners. Then write down all the things that could be associated with your chosen subject area, and try to group them under some headings.

- *Will all of these headings feature in your teaching?*

- *What will you choose to include, what will you leave out?*

- *Might your choices be different under different circumstances?*

- *What teaching methods would you use?*

- *How will you evaluate the success of your curriculum?*

Try to justify the choices you make.

Where did this activity take you? What kind of issues were you looking at? Do you think it is more important to learn about some practical issues? Were you looking at the skills that were involved in your subject? Did you decide to explore the social and political context of your subject? Did you discard some aspects because they were too expensive/could not get funded?

As we can see from the activity above what *could* be part of a curriculum and what eventually and *actually becomes* part of any curriculum is not fixed or arbitrary, but rather the result of a complex interplay of interests and perspectives – for example, political, social, economic, ideological ones. Therefore a curriculum is the result of deliberate choices and it is not neutral, but socially constructed and ultimately political.

What interests shape a curriculum?

Jürgen Habermas, a German sociologist and philosopher, suggests that the pursuit of knowledge derives from three different kinds of basic human instincts (he calls them 'knowledge constituent interests').

1 **Control**: This is the kind of knowledge that helps people to control and predict their environment. Many of the skills that are needed to 'make things work', from learning how to grow vegetables to operating a computer, will fall into this category.

2 **Understanding**: This is the kind of knowledge that helps us understand the social world we inhabit and make judgements about the actions that we take.

3 **Emancipation**: This is the kind of knowledge that helps us to question, to develop a critical position towards the social world and explore the struggles and power relationships that exist within it, as *knowledge is not just for controlling and understanding, but equally for criticising* (Crossley, 2005).

Habermas does not see these interests to be in a hierarchical order, but each of the underlying knowledge constituent interests will shape the curriculum in very specific ways. Let us look at them in turn.

Control

Starting with Habermas' first knowledge constituent interest Grundy (1987) outlines how a curriculum pursuing a 'control' agenda is primarily based on the development of skills. The application of skill and the human action resulting from it is closely related to 'production' in the widest sense. The end result or outcome of this kind of curriculum will ultimately be dependent on an original idea or pattern of what was to be created. The judgement as to whether the end result is good or satisfactory will then depend on how closely it resembles the original idea. Grundy here makes a comparison with craftspeople who will use their technical skill to create a product that needs to conform to some set and agreed standard. If a carpenter sets out to make a table and ends up with a chest of drawers instead, the person commissioning the table will not be too pleased, even if the chest of drawers is the most beautifully crafted piece of furniture there ever was! Similarly, if you are meant to make a cake and end up with a delicious soup you will be judged on the failure of the cake-making efforts, not on the success of the soup. What we can see here is that craftspeople can only apply their skills in particular, predetermined ways if their action is to be regarded as successful.

This raises a number of important issues, both about the distribution of power and control in the process and the professional autonomy of the craftsperson.

The creator of the original idea (or the standard) is not normally the person who is charged with implementing it, therefore a professional will only have a limited range of options how to go about the task. So, returning to our doomed joiners and cake-makers above – they will have some opportunity to display their specific skill, say in their choice of materials and ingredients, but their efforts are essentially 'reactive' to the original idea and may become obsolete if the nature of the commissioning ideas and demands change. Extending this example to an educational setting, it becomes clear that outcomes and targets are usually set neither by the professional tasked with achieving them, nor indeed by the learner who will have little or no say over what should be learned and in what way.

A curriculum that is control or outcome oriented requires a particular kind of professional who will have the skill to implement predetermined objectives. The power in this case rests quite firmly with those who set the agenda, and as pointed out above, not the learner and not the professional. Similar to the commissioners of tables and cakes, the ultimate sanction is to withhold payment if the outcome is not achieved. To ensure the exact implementation of the 'plan' or the original 'idea' there is a need to control the learner, the learning environment and the learning content as much as possible, so all elements of the learning process need to be predetermined. This often results in meticulous step-by-step guides, ensuring that there is not too much room for variation or interpretation on behalf of the teacher. An example of this was the national training programme for Connexions personal advisors, which worked to a very specific brief that was replicated to every small detail by all training providers across the country.

ACTIVITY **4.2**

In your workplace or placement, look at a piece of work that has set educational outcomes or targets.

- *Who has set the targets/outcomes?*

- *What do you think of them?*

- *What do the learners think of them?*

- *How are these outcomes achieved?*

- *How have you been prepared for this work?*

- *How much scope is there to set different outcomes?*

- *How is the work evaluated?*

- *What are the consequences of not achieving the predetermined outcomes?*

The particular distribution of power arising from a skill or outcome based curriculum also has an impact on how knowledge is regarded. What should be learned becomes separated both from the learner and teacher – it becomes a commodity:

> *Knowledge is objective, 'bounded' and 'out there'. Classroom knowledge is often treated as an external body of information, the production of which appears to be independent of human beings. From this perspective, human knowledge is viewed as being independent of time and place: it becomes universalised, a historical knowledge. Moreover it is expressed in a language which is basically technical and allegedly value free . . . Knowledge then becomes not only countable and measurable, it also becomes impersonal.*

> (Giroux, 1981 in Grundy, 1987, p34)

Regarding knowledge as independent of its context will make it look neutral and mask the particular and subjective choices that have been made. More importantly, knowledge of this kind can be transferred wholesale without involving the learner and becomes easily testable, or as Habermas would say, controllable. The Brazilian adult educator Paulo Freire called this approach to education and knowledge the 'banking system of education'. In this system Freire would argue that learners are treated like empty vessels who can be filled with knowledge – for safe-keeping like a safety deposit box in a bank – to be accessed again, of course in its original state, in the shape of examinations.

Understanding

Let us move on to Habermas' second knowledge constituent interest 'Understanding' and see how this disposition affects a curriculum differently from what we have discussed above.

The act of 'understanding' is essentially different from the act of applying a skill. First, it requires both learners and teachers to engage with the subject matter or the learning process and they therefore both become active participants. Rather than act in accordance with a preconceived idea they both interact with the subject matter which shifts the distribution of power more evenly onto all participants. The role of the teacher or professional is less to transfer knowledge but more to create an environment where learning can take place. *This means learning not teaching will become the central concern of the teacher* (Grundy, 1987, p69).

Second, there are implications about the nature of knowledge and the process of learning. Knowledge that is generated though a process of understanding is not separated from the learner. Instead theory and knowledge evolve out of a process of interaction and are tested and revised in the learners' reality and experience. Understanding and learning in this context are guided by practical wisdom, both by the learner and teacher, about 'how best to proceed'. As a result the outcomes of the learning process require professional judgement and will not be predictable in the way they might be within a skill-based curriculum.

Looking at the curriculum from a 'control' and 'understanding' perspective, the differences can be summarised as follows.

	Control	**Understanding**
Learner	Mainly passive recipient. Little control over what is being learned.	Actively shapes and engages with theory and knowledge.
Knowledge	'Objective', detached, measurable.	Develops through a process of interaction and is tested and revised through the experience of the learner.
Teacher/ Professional	Delivers according to a 'plan'. Limited professional autonomy.	Provides environment for learning. Interacts with learner and knowledge .
Process	Transfers predetermined knowledge. Process is often highly regulated.	Learning is a two-way process. Interaction.
Outcomes	Usually set by external agency (commissioners). Not set by learners and teachers. Easily testable.	Arise out of the learning process. Outcomes are generated through the learning process and are not predictable.

Figure 4.1 Curriculum control vs. understanding

ACTIVITY 4.3

Look at your own learning experiences.

- *Can you identify learning experiences that followed a skills-based curriculum with preset areas of knowledge?*

- *Can you think of occasions when this knowledge was useful to you and can you think of occasions when you had to learn things that you did not understand the use/relevance of?*

- *What could have been done to make the learning more relevant for you?*

- *How do you feel about the activities in this book?*

- *You are often invited to reflect on areas of theory and relate them to your own practice. What do you think about this method?*

Your reflections in the above activity are likely to have provided you with examples for both kinds of learning and Habermas agrees that there is a need for both approaches. However, he claims that there is generally an overemphasis on the first knowledge constituent interest as it reflects a dominance of what is regarded as 'scientific' enquiry over other methods of understanding and exploring the social world (scientific in this context refers to 'positivist' enquiry that will only value knowledge that comes from measurement and observable phenomena). Habermas would argue that even the knowledge constituent interests of understanding and emancipation themselves are influenced by an overarching need for control and therefore *Positivism marks the end of the theory of knowledge. In its place emerges the philosophy of science* (Habermas, 1987, p67).

Habermas' view that knowledge is largely shaped by the demands of scientific (positivist) enquiry and the accompanying need to control is echoed in the writing of the French sociologist and philosopher Michel Foucault. Foucault is particularly interested in the way knowledge is classified and the rationale behind the methods of classification. It is worth remembering that Foucault started his professional life as a psychologist and many of his examples are therefore located in the medical and natural sciences field. However, his thinking can easily be transferred to other settings. Foucault points out that the interests in science and medicine for example do not arise out of a vacuum, but rather as a response to and within the context of the social world and its issues at the time. What does this tell us about knowledge and its classification? It suggests that classifications interact reflexively with the way social problems are perceived within society. One of the examples Foucault cites is how definitions of normality and 'madness' shift depending on the potential for the integration of dissenting behaviour. So, the difference between 'normal' and 'not normal' – mad – lies primarily in the way the resulting behaviour poses a problem for society. The labelling process, and often in the case of defined mental illness the resulting institutionalisation and segregation, can become a vehicle for control. Part of this control will then be the development of research and scientific enquiry of this socially constructed phenomenon, which in turn will become a method of classification in its own right as *possible objects of social scientific knowledge often emerge against the backdrop of social problems, which, in turn are problems of social order and control, that is problems of 'power'* (Crossley, 2005, p224).

A contemporary example of this could be the way young people are categorised and labelled as NEET (not in education, employment or training). It can be argued that this category has arisen as society has developed more skills-based employment patterns and is increasingly operating in a global environment. At a time when there was an abundance of unskilled or low-skilled employment opportunities, for example, the fact that young people were leaving school without qualifications or further training would not have posed the same issues for Britain's ability to compete on international markets. The category NEET, which would not have been a logical or sensible one before, has now become one that categorises young people visibly around the social and economic issues that they present for society. A further example is the way young people are clustered around issues like teenage pregnancy or their drinking behaviour. As identifiable categories these young people can then become objects of enquiry and, as a result, often focused, remedial measures.

ACTIVITY **4.4**

Look at the target groups for your work.

- *Are these new groupings?*

- *What are the issues that unite them?*

- *What are the social problems that are associated with these groups?*

- *What is the self-identity of these groups?*

- *Are these groups homogeneous?*

- *Who has made decisions that these groups should be classified as such?*

- *Who benefits from these classifications?*

- *What are the drawbacks?*

This activity is likely to have highlighted a number of issues with reference to the way target groups are arrived at. For example you might have found that the 'labels' given to groups are not the ones its members identify with. Or the targets might not be in keeping with what the people involved think the most important issues are. Others might have felt that the focus on 'problems' does not allow you to explore a group's strength.

Before we move on to a curriculum concerned with Habermas' third knowledge constituent interest 'emancipation' we are going to explore the concept of hegemony and theories of capital that can help us understand how inequality is maintained and provide good starting points for a curriculum that is concerned with social justice.

Hegemony

Hegemony is a term originally coined by Lenin, but that is now usually associated with the Italian thinker Antonio Gramsci. As a Marxist, Gramsci was imprisoned by the Italian fascists for a lot of his short adult life which did not deter him from continuing his thinking and writing and many of his ideas and thoughts can be found in his Prison Notebooks.

Hegemony was originally used in an economic sense describing the dominance of one (small) social class but it is now used more widely to describe the dominance (or rule) of one group over another. With this concept Gramsci added a further dimension to Marxist explanations of dominance and coercion through economic and structural means. Domination through coercion has limitations as those who are oppressed and who are usually in the majority could attempt to resist and overthrow the dominant class. Dominance is maintained much more effectively through what he calls intellectual and moral leadership, through which the consent of those in less powerful positions is secured. Gramsci suggests that those who are oppressed develop a 'false' consciousness through viewing the world from the perspective of the powerful. As a result the circumstances of their oppression appear normal and it becomes 'common sense' that there should be differences in power relationships, different privileges, life chances, etc. This kind of common sense can then serve very effectively to mask the imbalances of power that exist in society by making them feel and sound natural and inevitable. Domination therefore is held in place by the consent of the powerless, rather than by coercion of the powerful. So if we are seeking ways of tackling inequalities it is necessary to explore some of the underlying beliefs and ideas that tend to maintain unequal power relationships.

ACTIVITY **4.5**

In the coming week try to listen specifically to the kinds of statements people make that ultimately legitimise inequalities. Look out for statements made about individuals themselves, such as 'I am hopeless at writing', 'I have never been any good at . . .' and for those that are made about groups in society: 'this is not for the likes of us', 'not everybody can become a . . .'

Look at the statements you have heard. How common are they? What do they tell you about people's perception of themselves? Can you detect any general views about the aspirations and expectations of particular sections in society? Do you believe these statements?

Theories of capital

Although the concept of capital was originally associated with **economic resources**, it has now become more widely used to describe a range of other resources that people can utilise to further their goals. In recent years the most prominent discussion has centred on the idea of **social capital** and it has become a feature of contemporary writing within social theory. Although elements of the theoretical concepts surrounding social capital have featured in earlier writings it is the writing of Robert Putnam (2000), that appears to have elicited the widespread and popular response to social capital theory.

Social capital thinking has now permeated a wide range of policy initiatives and also features prominently in academic writing and research, linking social capital to outcomes in a broad range of areas, such as education, health, community safety and economic growth. And yet the concept appears to remain very loosely defined and to have acquired a number of different, partially contradictory and ambiguous meanings. Common to most writers, including Putnam, is a reference to 'norms, trust and networks', as the essential prerequisites for a flourishing infrastructure that allows communities to prosper (2000). Although Putnam's work has attracted considerable controversy and criticism it is his claim that social capital is declining that is most enduring and provides the focus for a sustained interest in, both academically and in policy terms, how to halt or reverse this decline. The current emphasis on volunteering, as an extension of an equally prominent citizenship debate for example, can be viewed within this context.

Generally, social capital is categorised into three different forms: bonding, bridging and linking (Gilchrist, 2004). Bonding in this context refers to the links that groups develop among themselves; bridging refers to links between groups; and linking captures the relationships that go beyond peer boundaries and immediate spheres of influence. Most of the literature portrays social capital in a positive light and there is generally little recognition that social capital can have negative as well as positive outcomes, as, for instance, strong bonds within groups can create insider and outsider scenarios and the trust within groups can increase mistrust and exclusion of others.

However, there is a different version of social capital, and its associated concept of social space, suggested by Pierre Bourdieu, that is particularly helpful for our discussion on education. Even though Bourdieu essentially regards social capital as the networks that individuals can draw on as a personal resource, he also places social capital within the context of other forms of resources (such as economic, cultural, symbolic capital) that interact with each other and position a person in social space (Bourdieu, 1984). As these forms of capital are not evenly distributed within society, an exploration of social capital suggests a structural perspective on the availability of resources. Social capital therefore transcends the importance it can have for individuals as it refers to the distribution and maintenance of privilege within society and thus the collective experience of power and (dis)advantage of particular groups. Research on the decline of social capital tends to concentrate on individual inclination but social capital and engagement is also affected by the composition of the neighbourhoods where people live. Poverty, for example, inhibits civic engagement such as voting behaviour and engagement in national political affairs, but often generates many instances of people attempting to redress inequalities locally. As a result, less powerful groups may well have a rich range of social networks, but their relative positioning and status is unlikely to yield access to the 'friends in high places', or display features of 'linking' social capital that Bourdieu regards as a cornerstone for the acquisition and maintenance of privilege and influence.

For the purpose of this chapter, and returning to the subject of education, it is Bourdieu's ideas on cultural and symbolic capital that warrant some closer inspection.

Cultural capital, as the term suggests, is related to the cultural resources that a person, or more importantly groups of people have to secure privileges in society. Cultural capital and its relationship to education play a crucial role here. As we have seen above, what counts as public knowledge is socially determined. Moreover, the value that is associated with different kinds of cultural traits distinctly favours particular social groups and helps to secure, maintain and develop social advantage and disadvantage. Bourdieu suggests that this works in the following way.

From an early age, middle class children tend to have access to different kinds of cultural resources and pursuits, for example they are more likely to go to the theatre, have music lessons, own books. Bourdieu refers to this as cultural capital in its objectified form. When children go to school, the school curriculum in the widest sense (in terms of what is learned, the methods that are being used to teach and the ways learning is evaluated and tested) will favour children with a middle class background and as a result they are more likely to succeed and gain the qualifications that are likely to secure them better paid and more influential jobs – the effect of cultural capital therefore become institutionalised. Cultural capital interacts with what Bourdieu refers to as 'symbolic capital', to become cultural capital in its embodied form, i.e. people from advantaged backgrounds will display cultural traits such as 'refined' manners and 'educated' accents which will immediately define them as belonging to privileged groups.

In terms of power, equality and education cultural capital considerations have far reaching effects.

The advantage that has been systematically secured and socially constructed can easily be portrayed as natural and inevitable divisions within society. Similar to what we have considered in the section on hegemony, unequal power relationships arising from constructed educational disadvantage become 'normal' and acceptable.

The education system plays a powerful role in supporting privileged groups within society to exercise control over definitions of what constitutes worthwhile knowledge, what is considered to be 'good' taste, a refined lifestyle and so on, thus ensuring that the resulting privileges remain within a small selection of society. Bourdieu's writings on 'taste' are particularly revealing in this context. The judgement of what is considered to be a sign of refinement or vulgarity will remain with those in powerful positions: a lot of gold jewellery on a 'well-dressed' woman on the Cote d'Azur will be regarded as a sign of good standing within society; the same adornment on a young woman in a track suit on a council estate in the north-east of England might well not elicit the same esteem in the wider world. Being interested in and being able to talk about literature and art for example is assigned a higher status then for example being able to talk about pop music. Not only is the school curriculum generally organised in a way that makes it easier to succeed for those who have the more highly regarded skills, these skills will also give a higher status to their bearers. In order to maintain the privileges and esteem that are associated with certain skills, 'talents' and resulting lifestyles, the symbolic value is subject to change and the lines of distinctions are likely to shift. For example, going abroad, once the prerogative of the well-off, is now affordable for a much wider range of social classes. As a result new distinctions need to be made, for example which destinations are regarded to be 'common' and which remain desirable.

ACTIVITY 4.6

Briefly study the people you work with.

- *What kinds of interests do they have?*

- *What kinds of skills do they have?*

- *How do they value the skills they have?*

- *How are these skills valued within society overall?*

- *What kinds of 'doors' do these skills open?*

You are likely to have found that skills can come in different categories of usefulness. Some skills have a universally recognised value that allows people access to jobs and further education for example. Other skills have a lot of value within a certain domain but not much outside it – women's domestic skills could be in this category. Others can be put to use to earn money. Others again have value within certain cultures and social classes.

A further dimension of Bourdieu's writing that is helpful in understanding the idea of capital is how different kinds of capital interact with and compound both privilege and disadvantage. As mentioned earlier, these mechanisms do not apply randomly to individuals but account for the systematic relative positioning of groups of people within society. For example, let us look at how economic capital interacts with cultural and symbolic capital: a person's standing and opportunities in society are different if they are economically poor, but are considered to be cultured and speak with a refined accent. If this person has also been to a 'good' school and comes from a privileged family they are also likely to have more influential social capital, i.e. know privileged people whose resources might be drawn on to increase status, secure own privileges and so on. In Bourdieu's terms these people are 'capital rich'. Similarly, there are people who have money, but few of the other sources of capital, and of course there are groups of people who score very high or very low on all counts.

What can we do about inequality and education?

The issues of inequality and disadvantage are not unfamiliar in educational discourses and are recurring themes in educational policy. Jane Thompson (1997), using the example of the position of women in adult education, has classified educational responses into the following categories:

- total ignorance;

- philanthropy;

- measured acceptance;

- freedom from control.

Let us see how these responses work in practice.

The first option of course is to ignore inequality and to continue providing education that will explicitly or implicitly continue to disadvantage certain groups of people. The example from The National Institute of Adult Continuing Education (NIACE) given by Thompson relates the way adult education classes used to re-enforce stereotypical roles of women as homemakers and how the curriculum was almost exclusively determined by men, with little regard made to political movements. Adult education has traditionally been the only area of education where women were in the majority both as participants and part-time tutors. However, they remained largely absent in management, research and policy formulation roles. As a result women remained in the position of being the consumers of knowledge generated by men.

ACTIVITY **4.7**

- *What examples from your workplace can you think of where existing provision does not take into account the needs of particular groups in society?*
- *What reasons and explanations are given for this?*

The second approach Jane Thompson identifies as (latter-day) philanthropy. Inequalities are viewed as 'charitable causes' with attempts being made to give to the 'needy', but with the providers retaining the rights to determine who is 'deserving' and who is 'non-deserving'. As with the philanthropic approach Jane Thompson also points out that the givers are likely to benefit at least as much, or in some cases even more, from the relationship. In some cases the gesture can be viewed as more important than its success and can also serve as a useful tool to deflect anger and rebellion. A particular feature of this approach is that, rather than addressing the systematic exclusion of certain groups within society, practices are designed to alleviate the perceived deficiencies of individuals. People are then portrayed as the problems they present rather than the strength they bring. Educational provision is designed to address the symptoms rather than the underlying causes of social issues. Many community and youth workers talk about how the current emphasis on meeting predetermined targets (or mainly having to follow a 'control' oriented curriculum) does not allow them to work to the actual needs of the people they work with and how they feel constrained in their professional judgement.

ACTIVITY **4.8**

What examples can you think of where your own professional judgement about how to work with, for example, a young person conflicted with the targets you had to work to?

The next approach Jane Thompson outlines refers to a measured/controlled acceptance that there is a need to address inequality – resulting in 'respectable' measures. The respectability is achieved by changing the language to more acceptable forms – instead of liberation and oppression for example we refer to disadvantage and equality of opportunity. Here we can see also some re-definition of what constitutes an acceptable curriculum by for example incorporating black people's and women's perspectives on history and health. Similarly there are some additions to a traditional curriculum, such as assertiveness, women's self-defence, sexuality and women's non-traditional skills. What we can see here is that some recognition is given to the fact that there are groups in society that a traditional curriculum and mainstream provision does not serve too well. However, the remaining power structures remain essentially intact, as are definitions of excellence and success, who employs teachers and controls the resources. Ledwith (2005) points out that hegemony can take flexible forms and that part of its survival can be ensured by showing that criticisms are taken on board, but without threatening the foundations of dominant relationships. *Just because courses are attended by women, taught by women and are about women, does not in itself make them feminist* (Thompson, 1988, p191).

ACTIVITY **4.9**

Look at your work and the targets you work to.

- *Can you identify measures that would fit into one or more of the categories outlined above?*

- *Is there other educational work that you do or are involved in that does not fit into any of these categories? Explain what you think the difference is.*

Freedom from control or the pursuit of liberation

Jane Thompson, as the final response, talks about freedom from control. Freedom from control is closely related to Habermas' third knowledge constituent interest 'emancipation' which we referred to earlier in this chapter and we will now explore in more detail. This will locate our discussion in the realm of critical pedagogy, as *there is not a great deal of historical precedent to support the view that patriarchy can be transformed by sweet reason and persuasion* (Thompson, 1997, p80). So what options are there?

Education concerned with transformation is often referred to as critical or liberation pedagogy and is essentially an extension of the curriculum concerned with understanding. One of the main theorists associated with this approach is the Brazilian educationalist Paulo Freire. He defines liberation pedagogy as a *process by which individuals come to see and understand the structures which stand between them and becoming 'fully human', that is unexploited and whole* (1972). To understand the essential features of a curriculum concerned with transformation and liberation we are going to look at the essential aspects again and see how they are different from what we have explored before:

- the learning process (problem posing);

- the 'teachers' (intellectuals);

- knowledge (useful to the learner);

- outcomes (committed action – praxis).

Problem posing

Paulo Freire was influenced by the writings of Antonio Gramsci and it is useful to return to Gramsci's thoughts on hegemony. As we have discussed earlier, it is people's beliefs, thoughts, the 'unquestioned' and 'taken for granted' that secure hegemony and privilege. The first step in effecting change therefore is to start questioning some of these beliefs.

Let us look in a little more detail at how this form of questioning could actually happen. Freire (1972) suggests that the starting point for transformative learning needs to be the context people find themselves in and the issues that people feel strongly about – these are the issues that people 'speak about with excitement, hope, fear, anxiety or anger'. Sometimes these issues are called 'generative themes' precisely because they are such good starting points for conversation.

The process of questioning itself Freire refers to as 'problem posing'. Through the process of problem posing the themes that people feel strongly about are explored in some depth in order to go beyond the 'taken for granted'. This could focus on how ideas and beliefs were developed, where and from whom people had learned them and how their views fit into a wider scenario. This kind of questioning is then taken into increasingly wider contexts, starting with the self, the family, the community and finally making the link to underlying global issues.

In terms of outcome a praxis oriented curriculum helps oppressed groups to understand their oppression systemically, so individual experiences are linked to the structures in society that maintain them. It can link one form of oppression with the experience of other oppressed groups. The learning therefore goes beyond understanding one's own position – for example, from a class, gender or race perspective – and has a wider focus on learning about oppressive structures in general.

It is here where the difference between the process of consciousness raising and the process of 'conscientisation' that Freire highlights in his writing becomes apparent. Both concepts deal with 'subjugated knowledge', but 'consciousness raising' will empower people on an individual level whereas 'conscientisation' will develop the critical capacity to understand oppression systemically and link it to social action. This process essentially extends learning from the individual perspective and forges links to other groups, helping people to seek collective solutions in solidarity with others.

CASE STUDY

The abseil off the Tyne Bridge

One year to mark International Women's Day, a mass abseil off the bridge over the river Tyne was organised in Gateshead. About 180 women of different backgrounds, abilities and disabilities, ages and sizes took part. For many weeks afterwards it was almost impossible to go anywhere in Gateshead without meeting people who in some way had been involved or touched by the event and many conversations were started as a result. Almost without fail the starting point here was that people talked about having done something that they never thought they would do or having witnessed somebody else do something that they thought was near impossible. The animated way this was talked about provided many generative themes that could be explored in a number of different directions. Here are some of the most common responses and the way these were developed into critical discussions.

I am really timid, me, I would never do anything like this.

Why do you think you are timid? Who told you so? Are there times in your life when you are not timid? What is different about these times? What would happen if you were behaving differently?

This conversation developed into an exploration of women's roles and positions in society, who benefited from women not leaving their roles and how women's perception of themselves and what they are allowed to do is shaped. A separate strand developed into the roles of older women and the limitations and expectations they were experiencing. Again, discussions developed into how older women were treated within their families, how they were portrayed in the media and how much space society overall allowed them to occupy. As one woman put it: All my life I have seen myself as a timid woman; perhaps I am not timid after all, perhaps I have been made timid, perhaps other people prefer me to be timid, but my future could be so different if I saw myself as a courageous woman.

I always thought you had to be dead fit to do anything like this.

This conversation developed into general perceptions of sports and outdoor activities, how the media portrays people with disabilities. The latter in particular focused on what were real and physical limitations and what were imagined/constructed ones. How were the latter arrived at? Who benefited from these limitations and who had an interest in maintaining them?

This sort of thing is impossible for the likes of me.

This was maybe the most common response and the sentiments were expressed in a number of different ways – almost without fail all the women who took part never thought that people like them would abseil off the Tyne Bridge. This raised issues about social class and how aspirations were determined by what people felt they were 'entitled to'.

A further, slightly different, conversation arose out of the statement that some women claimed that they suffered from an extreme fear of heights, so they were 'structurally' unsuited for an activity like this. However, faced with the fact that they had actually just managed to abseil despite their fears led to many conversations about what else there might be in this world that they never thought they could/would do. This in turn led to many conversations about perceptions of self, how these were formed, how they are maintained and how they affect daily lives. As a result many conversations centred on lost and unfulfilled dreams, hopes and aspirations. This moved on to a more detailed analysis of what the perceived obstacles are and what it was that made the impossible possible on that rainy Sunday in March. Women now began to analyse what helped them to overcome their fears and transfer these to other aspects of their life experiences. Rather than locate the obstacles in themselves some women were now looking at past experiences to try to analyse what helped or hindered them. Others started talking about how circumstances, environments and support structures could be changed to allow them to do what they were really aspiring to.

As we can see here the actual experience of the abseil posed a concrete challenge to many strongly held beliefs. Through the process of questioning women started to look at their lives in a number of different time-frames. As a result constructions of the past were 'rewritten' and new aspirations for the future were emerging. This was then linked to an analysis of power structure, both as a gendered process and more generally, while widening the context from the personal, their communities and society in general.

Intellectuals

Freire points out that questioning the status quo and challenging existing beliefs are not processes that start 'naturally', but that they depend on some form of intervention. This intervention will ultimately rest with those people who use their intellectual powers to analyse and question the dominant views that support hegemonic perspectives. Gramsci broadly calls these people 'intellectuals' but distinguishes between two different kinds – 'traditional' and 'organic'. Traditional intellectuals in this context are those who might not belong to oppressed groups themselves but who, because of their commitment to social justice, can play useful and important roles. They can provide environments and circum-stances for critical reflection (Ledwith, 2005), support groups and become allies. However, their impact is limited as long-term, sustainable transformation relies on the active involvement of those who are affected by their oppression. This is an important distinction to make as people are not seen as participants but the agents of change. These people Gramsci would call organic intellectuals, that is people who come from 'within', people who have an organic commitment to their neighbourhood and a sense of belonging while they are also capable of contributing an outside perspective, or to *see the local in terms of the global and the global in terms of the local* (Smith, 1994, p16). They typically question the status quo and involve others in this process. Their role is to bridge the gap between inside and outside perspectives, by analysing power relationships, asking questions, working with people's values and encouraging new and different ways of being and thinking.

Look at the communities you are familiar with.

- *Can you locate the intellectuals within them?*

- *Who are the people who are from the 'outside' and have important functions creating environments for questioning and challenging the 'taken for granted'? What do they actually do?*

- *Who are the people from 'within' – what are their roles, what do they do?*

- *What do you think the differences between these roles are?*

Knowledge

Knowledge that is generated through an emancipatory curriculum is not a 'commodity', it is not decided on beforehand and separated from the learner; instead it arises out of the process of learning itself. As we have seen before, a control oriented curriculum essentially starts with the end, in the way that the projected learning outcomes are the starting point for the learning process. In a praxis orientated curriculum what is learned arises from the process of questioning. The starting point here is the experience of the learner and learning is negotiated in a dialogical form between the learner and the teacher, who in Freirean terms become 'co-investigators' in the learning process. The learner therefore ultimately takes control of the learning outcomes and the resulting knowledge, the value of which is defined by the usefulness to the learner and its capacity to promote social change. Some writers have referred to this kind of knowledge as 'really useful knowledge'.

ACTIVITY *4.11*

First, think about the learning in your life.

- *Can you identify really useful knowledge – i.e. knowledge relevant to you that has helped you to make changes in your life?*

- *What were the issues you were learning about?*

- *What were the circumstances?*

- *Who helped with your learning?*

Now move on to your professional life and the people you work with.

- *Can you identify learning that would help/have helped people make changes in their own lives and in their local community?*

Of course, one thing we need to remember when looking at 'really useful knowledge' is that the dominant view on knowledge and its value will mirror what we have been discussing in terms of hegemony and the prevalence of scientific/positivist approaches. Many people therefore might take it for granted that learning will not be relevant or useful to them and reject the idea of education making a contribution to their lives and others like them. One memorable example of this was when I was undertaking a survey on what kind of adult education classes were needed/wanted in an ex-mining community. One older woman laughed out loud at me and gently informed me that she did not need adult education, she needed to change the washer in her tap. What does this response indicate? Here are a few interpretations: adult education classes are for other people; adult education is a luxury; the learning content is not relevant; you cannot change the content; there are pressing issues in one's life that learning cannot solve?

However, following the principles of 'really useful knowledge' and that of committed action below, a whole range of opportunities arise to look at the issues that were important in this woman's life and others in her position, and work to develop a curriculum that would meet her needs.

Committed action – praxis

This final aspect of an emancipatory curriculum is often referred to as praxis, or committed action – with the aim to transform unequal power relationships. Praxis depends on a reflexive relationship between reflection and action; that is, one builds upon the other.

ACTIVITY **4.12**

Return to the case study about the abseilers. Re-read the various conversations that arose from the experience and the issues raised as a result. Can you imagine what form 'committed action' could take?

Carol Packham (2008) drawing on Thompson (2001) suggests that informal learning and the resulting action can impact on change on three different levels:

- personal/individual;

- cultural/institutional;

- societal/structural.

Let us see how our abseilers developed their committed action and look at some examples.

Many of the women began to look at their personal circumstances and talked about making small changes in their personal lives. (We talk about similar processes in Chapter 3.) For some women this meant deciding to take more time for themselves, for others it resulted in negotiating a different way of doing household chores with their families.

On another level some women began to look at the things they wanted to do and analyse the obstacles they were facing. Rather than accept the limitations that they had thought were 'given' they started to question and challenge. For example, some women talked about wanting to get involved in more education and training but felt they could not because they either had childcare responsibilities or they did not have the confidence because of their lacking educational qualifications. They approached the local college and raised the issue of more flexible childcare and in other cases achieved that some courses were delivered locally in their community centres. The latter also had the effect that the educational needs of other people within their communities were discussed and more effective negotiations with educational providers began.

Looking at the section on intellectuals again, it is clear how the actions described above had been initiated and helped along by a range of different people. In some cases it was the community and youth workers who kept the conversations and dialogue going and often played vital roles by listening and encouraging less prominent voices to be heard. On other occasions they worked with groups on common issues to identify ways forward. However, as much of the impetus for change came from 'within' as group members started challenging the conditions that they felt were constraining them while also using their groups to provide much needed support to develop their action.

Working in groups offers a further dimension for emancipatory learning (see also Chapter 5). Community and youth work practice is based on group work and will see the interactions and relationships within them as the primary focus for informal education. Through this they will aim to create the conditions that any group can become what Knowles (in Smith, 1994, p111) calls a *laboratory of democracy, a place where people can learn to live co-operatively*. As has been shown there are groups which have been formed around common issues and concerns which may find collective expression in the forms of services they provide and how they relate to the wider world. This process in itself can be seen as contributing to an emancipatory curriculum, as they can give a voice to concerns of groups who may not take part in mainstream political life.

However, any group, whether it has an overtly political dimension or not, will have an associational structure which mirrors forms of democratic working. Through active participation in these, by taking positions within them, skills are gained which are transferable to other political processes. These 'laboratories of democracy' are crucial because, as Freire pointed out:

> people can only learn social and political responsibility by experiencing that
> responsibility, through intervention in the destiny of their children's schools, in the
> destinies of their trade unions and places of employment, through associations, clubs
> and councils, and in the life of their neighbourhoods, churches and rural communities,
> by actively participating in associations, clubs and charitable societies.

(Freire, 1974, p36)

However, groups and their associational life possess further emancipatory potential. A 'laboratory of democracy' can have a distinctly explosive dimension, as the practice of democracy also requires dealing with issues of power and voice between groups and within groups. The insistence to adhere to democratic principles has its limitations. Power is not just expressed in a capacity to take part in a democratic process, but much more through what 'goes on behind the scenes', who is perceived to have the right to voice their opinion and what structures are in place to stop opposition from emerging. So what we may also be looking at is a process of 'non-decision making', *where things do not cross people's minds, where questions go unasked, and demands are not made because people anticipate the reaction, or where people's wishes are simply ignored* (Smith, 1994, p124). In this way what happens in associational structures mirrors the distribution of power in the rest of society. So consequently every community association, however democratic its structure on the surface, often powerfully acts out the conflict between its older and younger users, women and men, people from different ethnic groups. This in turn is the starting point for social and political education in the widest sense – to work within groups and between groups, and where addressing the resistance to democratic working itself can become the focus for 'problem posing'.

C H A P T E R   R E V I E W

This chapter has looked at education and different ideas of how to construct a curriculum. In particular we have looked at the way learning and curricula are shaped by a number of different interests. As such, curricula can be designed to control as much as they can empower. How the different interests affect the respective aspects of the curriculum can be summarised in the table that follows.

	Control	Understanding	Emancipation
Learner	Mainly passive recipient. Little control over what is being learned.	Actively shapes and engages with theory.	Decides what is important to learn.
Knowledge	'Objective', detached.	Develops through a process of interaction and is tested and revised through the experience of the learner.	'Really useful' to the learners, has the capacity to effect change.
Teacher/ Professional	Delivers according to a 'plan'. Limited professional autonomy.	Provides environment for learning. Interacts with learner and knowledge.	Teachers and learners are 'co-investigators'.
Process	Transfer of predetermined knowledge. Process is often highly regulated.	Learning is a two-way process. Interaction. Judgement.	Problem posing, starting with the issues that are important in the lives of learners.
Outcomes	Usually set by external agency (commissioners). Not set by learners and teachers. Easily testable.	Arise out of the learning process. Outcomes are generated through the learning process and are not predictable.	Understanding of oppressive structures. Links to other oppressed groups. Committed action (praxis).

Figure 4.2 Curriculum interests overview

This chapter has also highlighted the power of ideas and how questioning the taken for granted is an essential starting point for those who want develop educational initiatives with a social justice agenda at its core. This involves critically examining the everyday ideas that shape our own and others' views on what is 'normal', 'inevitable' or 'changeable'. As educators, as 'traditional' or 'organic' intellectuals we therefore need to look at all aspects of the learning process and examine our roles as teachers and learners, be clear about the power relationships that shape the development of knowledge and focus on the needs, concerns and interests of learners first and foremost.

FURTHER READING

Grundy, S (1987) *Curriculum: product or praxis*. Lewis: Falmer.

Ledwith, M (2005) *Community development: a critical approach*. Bristol: The Policy Press.

Mayo, M (1997) *Imagining tomorrow: community adult education for transformation*. Leicester: NIACE (The National Institute of Adult Continuing Education).

Chapter 5
Group work

Frankie Williams

CHAPTER OBJECTIVES

This chapter will help you meet the following National Occupational Standards.

1.1.2 Enable young people to work effectively in groups

1.2.1 Plan, prepare and facilitate group work with young people

2.3.1 Promote equality of opportunity and diversity in your area of responsibility

2.3.2 Develop a culture and systems that promote equality and value diversity

2.3.3 Challenge oppressive behaviour in young people

3.3.1 Develop productive working relationships with colleagues

3.3.2 Develop productive working relationships with colleagues and stakeholders

It will also introduce you to the following academic standards as set out in the youth and community work benchmark statement (2009, QAA).

7.1
- Recognise and compare multiple, competing perspectives and challenge the status quo and dominant perspectives.
- Facilitate informal learning and community development using group work and a range of interpersonal skills.

7.2
- Identify discrimination, oppression and/or exclusion and be strategic in developing interventions to tackle these in different situations.

Introduction

Working in and with groups has been a stable feature of community and youth work and related social professions. However, many policy developments over the past years such as *Every Child Matters* and *Aiming High* have put much more emphasis on working with often specifically targeted individuals, aiming for very clearly specified outcomes.

Critics of this increasingly individualised approach tend to draw attention to the wide range of different benefits that come from approaching social issues from a collective perspective and these can be summarised under the following headings.

Associational life/social capital

Over the past 25 years the concept of social capital has become a prominent aspect of social theory. Although there are a number of different, sometimes even conflicting, definitions, it is the writing of Robert Putnam (2000) whose extensive study in the United States indicated how people had become disconnected from one another and how as a result social structures within communities had disintegrated. Although there is some disagreement on the nature and the usefulness of social capital as a concept, most writers and studies will see membership of organisations and associations as a prime indicator for the health of communal life. As a result, the support of the formation and maintenance of social groups remains an important professional intervention, especially for those who are concerned with the regeneration of local communities and neighbourhoods.

Democracy/citizenship

A further reason to look at working in groups lies in the considerable educational potential that groups hold. The interactions and relationships within groups offer rich opportunities for informal education if, as workers, we help create conditions where every group can become what Knowles calls a *laboratory of democracy, a place where people may have the experience of learning to live co-operatively* (in Smith, 1994, p111).

These 'laboratories of democracy' are crucial. Read again the words of Freire already quoted in the previous chapter:

> *people can only learn social and political responsibility by experiencing that responsibility, through intervention in the destiny of their children's schools, in the destinies of their trade unions and places of employment, through associations, clubs and councils, and in the life of their neighbourhoods, churches and rural communities, by actively participating in associations, clubs and charitable societies.*
>
> (Freire, 1974, p36)

Collective solutions/committed action

A further aspect of working with groups is that it allows us to work with people on common bonds. Many of the social issues that we come across in our work are not individual issues but tend to affect groups and whole sections of society. Rather than seeking individual solutions to what in essence are societal concerns, groups can work together to effect change in their own and their communities' lives. Informed and committed action – 'praxis' is seen as the essence of informal education (Smith 1994). This, it can be argued, runs counter to the current predominant concern with individual change and achievement. Moreover, many of the individual interventions are primarily focused on the perceived deficiencies of individuals, rather than their strengths. As can be seen later in this chapter working with groups can play a powerful role in recognising and building on the strengths that already exist within local communities.

This chapter therefore looks at groups from a number of different perspectives and highlights the essential roles that group workers can play in their work. It will explore 'why group work' and 'what makes a group' and will continue with an exploration of the relevant context for group work for community and youth practices drawing on work written from the 1960s onwards including Tuckman (1965), Button (1974), Belbin (1981), Mullender and Ward (1991), Gibson and Clarke (1995), Sharry (2001) and Preston-Shoot (2007). The concepts and methods explored within group work will reflect upon the equality and power issues associated with empowerment practices in the areas of inclusion, group communication, roles, leadership and evaluative tasks.

What is a group

Douglas (1978, 1993, 2000) has said there are three main components of groups: a common fate, a common social structure and people who interact face to face.

Groups are basic building blocks of society. It is through groups that society has historically accomplished tasks . . .

(Gibson and Clarke, 1995 p33)

Community and youth workers find themselves in two distinct roles with group work in their practice – primary groups are those made up of close friends, sometimes family members and well-formed and organically grown gangs/groups. These groups are ones that are not in the worker's control or creation. Secondary groups are newly made with coherent aims and have yet to become well established (Gibson and Clarke, 1995, pp39–40). It is therefore important that there is an understanding of what concepts, principles, values and dynamics underpin effective group work so that it enhances effective practice.

Most group work research has been undertaken within the social and psychodynamic field and has relied heavily on the understanding of the group leadership expertise being the driving force for the agenda and interpretation of the interactions. Community and youth group work has developed its own direction drawing on this key initial research from the social psychodynamics of the 1960s and 1970s. It has created a group work framework centred on aims and objectives, skills and approaches that are aligned with the principles of any effective youth and community work being driven from the concept of voluntary membership built within an empowering and voluntary membership approach.

Gibson and Clarke identify six key necessary factors inherent in effective groups:

* good respectful relationships;

* clear, agreed, transparent aims;

* individual accountability and self-generated responsibility;

* ability to make collective decisions;

* effective communication;

* clear, valued, understood roles (Gibson and Clarke, 1995, p35).

Workers therefore need to build their expertise of group work around these key factors whether as a group member, facilitator or leader:

> *working with groups is not a science but an art. It is an individual and creative process, and as with other creative and individual processes, one technique, one method, one exercise will not suit everyone. Each person has their own particular style, their own particular approach.*

(Gibson and Clarke, 1995, p3)

The following section explores the location of group work, different kinds of leadership, an analysis of different group work contexts, tools, skills and approaches that help group work in community and youth work practice.

Locating group work

It is always important to locate any practice within a political and policy framework. As an anti-oppressive practitioner involved in informal education, equality and social justice is at the heart of your professional duty. What does this mean? Is the focus for all community and youth work interventions to facilitate people's personal and social development? How might social justice and equalities impact upon this? What relevance would group work have to these two areas? The third consideration is the one that mainly relates to the policy context. What do the current policies say about people within their community contexts?

ACTIVITY 5.1

In your working practice, identify occasions when group work can and is being used effectively in the following three areas:

- *education, equalities, empowerment, social justice and anti-oppressive practice;*

- *young people's personal and social development;*

- *the policy context: for example,* Youth Matters, Every Child Matters *and* Community Cohesion.

You might find that you could recall many examples within group work with young people and community groups in relation to education and personal and social development but few in a policy context. This area more often occurs within staff group work rather than working with groups. You might also begin to see different types, styles and approaches of group work and ones where you adopt different roles and responsibilities. All these areas will be explored in this chapter in more detail later on. Initially it is important to think why do we bother with group work and what is important?

The following points highlight some of the main reasons for undertaking group work within community and youth work and also highlight the main underpinning practice values and principles:

- promote independence and self-reliance;

- promote social inclusion – individuals as citizens;

- promote community cohesion – individuals as collective citizens;

- promote choice;

- to address the 'moral panics' – for example, teenage pregnancy, respect, xenoracism, anti-social behaviour, gangs, fear, terror, mental health, criminality, school exclusion.

We now have a basic understanding of what groups we are familiar with in our work and some contextual issues relating to community activism and empowerment and basic reasons for group work. Now we can draw on what we already know about groups from our own practice. As groups are at the heart of all our lived experiences, it is important to acknowledge that our lived experiences of groups will be very different. We are different people with different cultural and family experiences and have accrued different professional knowledge. Also as group workers we must acknowledge the impact diversity and difference have on group behaviour and group learning. We will reflect on these issues throughout the chapter and in more depth in the section on power and leadership. Let us consider personal group experience.

ACTIVITY 5.2

Take five minutes on your own and note down your answers to these questions, thinking back to your own practice and issues of empowerment and disempowerment.

- *Positive and negative experiences of groups you belonged to.*

- *Have you ever led a group?*

- *What positive and negative experiences have you had in leading a group?*

- *What groups would you join and which would you avoid and why?*

Now reflect on your experiences and answer these questions.

- *What do you believe about groups?*

- *Who and what has shaped your beliefs about groups?*

- *What knowledge, values and understandings influence your group work practice?*

So what are the advantages and disadvantages of group work?

You have probably identified for yourself some of the following key issues that can disadvantage and advantage groups. Disadvantages could include the following.

- Groups can fail to empower individuals who then can become less confident than in a one-to-one interaction (this can link with people's experience of sexism, racism, etc.). Members can dominate or sub groups can form.

- Groups don't always pull in the same direction and can fragment even if they have a shared focus.

- Groups can reinforce stigma, stereotyping, prejudice and labelling.

All these disempowering issues can result in groups being unproductive and destructive. We will explore ways of working with these issues within Thompson's structural equity module with a solution-focused approach later on in this book.

Consider these possible advantages.

- Groups can provide a collective strength/voice that is much more dynamic and louder than an individual voice.

- Groups provide shared learning; shared stories; shared resistance to unjust power.

- Group learning can deepen knowledge and understanding as they can link the personal to the political. They can enable socio-emotional learning where individual or one-to-one interaction is limited.

- Groups can empower and generate positive social action and be a place for hope, belonging, learning, growth and giving and getting positive reward.

These advantages are caught within the bigger context of the three distinctions mentioned in the introduction of the associational life/social capital, democracy/citizenship and collective solutions/committed action.

The relevance for group work practice for community and youth workers includes the promotion of social change; a vehicle to build collective resilience, to empower, educate and transform. It can solve interpersonal, intrapersonal and intra- and inter- group problems. Groups have made positive differences in people's lives. They have been a vehicle for the exploration and support for strengthened interpersonal feelings and the action of belonging as well as a support for intrapersonal development. People have gained friendship; support; voice; hope; connectivity; and purpose. Individuals have learned new ways and believe in new possibilities (Mullender and Ward, 1991, Preston-Shoot, 2007).

Community and youth workers use group work in their practice because there is evidence that groupthink can energise individual think to create new ways of perceiving the world and alternative constructions for dealing with it. These alternative possibilities coincide with improved self-confidence, self-motivation and self-esteem. Effective community activists have worked in groups to enhance successful Community Involvement, e.g. Nottingham 'Who Cares' group and Derbyshire Coalition of Disabled People researched in the Mullender and Ward account (1991).

These benefits need to be energised by a practice that is underpinned by theoretical and ethical considerations. Your's and the user group's experiences are shaped by social divisions and dominant ideologies and cultural practices. Class, race, gender, sexuality, age and disability all include and exclude people; all pervade our everyday practices and all are influenced by elite hegemonic discourses. For example you might like to ponder on how might gender impact on people using groups to maximise their community involvement? To help group members explore the understanding of gender and sexism, this chapter will explore later on an exercise designed to highlight consciousness about gender issues in groups.

Primary and secondary group work

We are all probably part of primary and secondary groups. Secondary groups are those that we create with others or are invited to join; for example groups with transparent aims and objectives such as residents' groups, parents' support groups, campaigning groups, etc. and that often have plans for action and structural change. However, primary groups are those we have no choice in belonging to, such as family groups and social groups. They have a way of developing 'organically' with their actions and identity such as those with whom you go to events such as football matches, cinema, meals out, and for many young people they will be groups they 'hang about with'. For group workers these primary groups necessitate a need for different approaches and style of recording than secondary groups. Secondary groups are often formed by or facilitated by a worker whose role is to support, facilitate and empower the group members in their goals. This type of group work has been labelled 'Project' group work by Gibson and Clarke (1995) and is the more familiar approach associated with informal educators. There are well-documented approaches and tools available for workers in this group work that we will explore later on.

In the 1970s and 1980s Leslie Button's work with primary groups focused his research and youth work training material to support 'detached' young people's groups, devising a realm of training styles and techniques to aid working with these detached groups on the street and in centre drop ins. Often this work is now a natural part of the approach of detached workers working with young people on the streets. The following primary group enquiry is adapted from Button (1974).

ACTIVITY **5.3**

Think back to Activity 5.2 where you identified all the groups you were working with. Can you identify the secondary and primary groups? Take one of the primary groups (or, if you have been unable to recall one, then identify a primary group you could work with) and answer the following questions.

- *Who are the members of the group?*

- *Who holds the group together?*

- *What does the group do?*

- *Has the group a routine?*

- *What happens in a typical meeting?*

Think about your first encounter.

- *Where did you meet?*

- *What happened?*

- *Was that typical of your encounters with them?*

- *Think what the group members' answers to these questions would be. Do you think they would have different answers?*

This set of information will be useful for group workers who have just begun to work with a group. It provides useful observed evidence by the worker when reflecting on the group's progress and captures the group worker's initial and progressive assumptions of the group. The questions can be used to continue to reflect on the group work at later stages.

Self-enquiry

Button devised a series of proformas in regard to self-description by members of a group as well as for the group workers. He recognised that they could be used as a means to explore qualities, behaviours and personal feelings with the emphasis on self-description rather than evaluation. He created a series of appropriately worded questions for young people in groups based around issues of self-esteem, resilience, trust, change, emotions, e.g. patience and temper and compassion, friendships and individual ways of operating in groups. What is interesting is that this was created more than 30 years ago when the development of the group work profession was travelling in the opposite direction in that it was increasing the distance and distinctions between the expertise of the professional group worker and the group members' experience and 'control'. Button adhered to the principle that any group worker needs to experience and understand the group work process and techniques themselves as a member of a group before they could be an effective group member.

> *We are in an age of increasing choice, of individual morality, and of a democratic life in the sense that we are each of us freer to decide how we should behave. This adds greatly to the need for a capacity for personal judgement and action, and the pressures that emanate from powerful commercial interest and urgency to this need. Part of the deliberate purpose of the worker will be to help youngsters build a basis for that independent action. In this context it may be well to remind ourselves that personal means that we must also be in control of our own impulses.*

(Button, 1974, p68)

Button also insisted that any process instigated by the worker within a group was transparent and shared experience with the aim of building the member's self-esteem and autonomy. He promoted the use of the members' experiences and group reflections in order to enhance the human dynamics of both the leadership of the worker and participation of the young person so as to empower the group dynamic and individual's 'autonomy'.

> *The approaches of the group worker are becoming increasingly sophisticated and influential, and could be misused. There is a fine line between helping and manipulating, and the group worker's methods are equally available to the professional persuader. It is in part with the purpose of protecting young people and ourselves from our professional enthusiasm that we must keep central to our ambitions the growing autonomy of the individual.*

(Button, 1974, p68)

These days this type of enquiry within informal educators' group work has maybe become more sophisticated and routed in a named 'specific' approach, e.g. project group work and self-help models. His model and enquiry tools still provide very relevant and useful probing questions. He focused on creating exercises and shared dialogues with the individual group members' self-assessment of themselves and the group, rather than the outsider's 'professional' opinion. He also encouraged the same degree of reflection and enquiry by the worker of their own style and behaviours that they bring as a worker in a team of workers. He would argue that through this self-reflection, the worker and the young person can become more transparent about their contribution and effectiveness in their communication with their peers or as workers with 'adolescents'.

The following is an exercise of self-enquiry (adapted from Button, 1974).

ACTIVITY 5.4

As community and youth workers within a staff group, reflect on the following questions.

1 *How easy or difficult do I find it to open up conversation with members of the staff team about:*

   (a) daily tasks to be undertaken?

   (b) the way the team perform tasks?

   (c) our more personal feelings about what we are attempting to do?

2 *Do I fear rejection; am I prepared to risk rejection of or opposition to what I propose?*

3 *How conscious am I of the possibility of criticism (spoken or unspoken) of me? Does the fear of criticism in any way inhibit my action or approach?*

4 *How far do I need the approval of certain members of the team or can I go my own way?*

5 *Do I expect other people to accept what I say?*

6 *How do I respond to a crisis?*

7 *Can I get stuck into a difficult job or do I dither?*

8 *How resilient am I when things are difficult – can I keep pressing forward when others doubt?*

9 *What is my general level of persistence?*

10 *How do I feel about myself? For example:*

   (a) Am I a successful person, or a failure?

   (b) Am I a likeable person?

   (d) Am I an efficient person?

   (e) Am I an easy person to get on with?

11 *What kind of person am I?*

Self-enquiry is useful as this approach is dependent upon a certain level of self-awareness that is necessary for group workers to be effective about who they are and what strengths and weaknesses they have. Button's approach was to give workers in youth work training a similar group work experience as the groups they would be working with. Their peer group work training used the tools appropriately on themselves, as a peer group, before venturing out and working with these approaches and self-enquiries with the 'detached' groups. Understanding the group dynamics, roles and communication of group members aids the workers' ability to be effective and inclusive.

Group work process

Group work has developed professionally since the 1960s and is accepted as a means of essential practice for workers in people services across the spectrum of the more formal education and health institutions as well as the voluntary sector. Group work experimentation and research grew in the 1960s, so much so that in 1968 the New York Times declared it *the year of the group*. This era was an experimental time for developing group work creating new and different approaches of ways of dealing with the issues of empowerment and control with for example the creation of T groups and Gestalt groups, etc. (Sharry 2001). Research into and comprehension of group work, including Tuckman's model, has had to rely heavily on the medical psychological professional sector's work in therapy. Understanding Tuckman's (1965, 1984) identification of group stages of forming, storming, norming, performing and mourning has provided an essential knowledge of the internal mechanism of group processes to aid group work facilitators and leaders in work with the community and young people. Each section of Tuckman's stages needs different skills and emphasis by members and facilitators in order to appropriately support each stage.

Groupwork planning

Planning before starting a group or becoming involved in an existing group is an essential part of group work. The first question in working with secondary groups must be to decide if the aims for the work identified needs a group approach. If yes then what is its purpose as far as you are concerned? Why does the group need to be worked with? How can you get the people to work together, what venue is available and suitable, is the membership closed or open? Are you clear about your role as a worker? Is it to have one facilitator/leader, co-facilitators, group leadership, etc. and what resources do you have available for the work?

Storming
The first stage, storming, is about the process of group members identifying roles, strengths and skills. Storming is a high energy time when individuals test each other regarding agreed boundaries and 'rules'. This process helps to then clarify group goals and group rules. Gang rules are not formally agreed or formally negotiated; they evolve and are implicit by their nature. These goals and agreements can be made explicit using Leslie Button's (1974) group work thinking and that can help primary groups work together on their implicit issues. Button provided a framework for making roles and goals explicit to empower the group membership's individuality, autonomy and self-esteem.

Norming
The second stage of norming is a phase that enables the group to start planning for action, devising and agreeing sub goals, outcomes and outputs, etc. It becomes clear who does

what and when they will do it as goals become defined. This stage also benefits from the use of new tools and approaches such as those associated with solution-focused group work practice (for instance scaling questions, miracle questions, etc.), explored in Chapter 6. Brainstorming as a means to begin to illicit a detailed plan of action is another tried and tested approach by group workers.

Performing

The group now enters the performing stage where they begin to do the agreed action and keep engaging with monitoring their progress. The group energy is stable and sustainable.

Mourning/Ending

As the group completes its goals, they enter the mourning or ending stage as they become involved in ending which allows for the opportunity to summarise the evaluation process, tying up loose ends and acknowledging the group's and each other's achievements.

RESEARCH ACTIVITY

Pick two of your groups you have been working with for a while from the list you created earlier in this chapter and fill in evidence you can recall for each of five Tuckman stages they have gone through.

Stages	Factors	Group 1 evidence	Group 2 evidence
Forming	Preparing, setting up, establishing aims and purpose, getting to know each other, setting the scene, setting learning agreements, methods of working and timescales.		
Storming	Challenging roles and tasks and direction, differences of opinion raised.		
Norming	Coming to decisions on redefined roles and tasks and aims, establish norms and methods of communication, decision making and action plan.		
Performing	Carrying out and completing agreed tasks, flow of communication, effective decision making, valuing each other.		
Mourning/ ending	Finishing, tying up loose ends, acknowledging the journey, evaluating the process.		

Figure 5.1 Recording evidence against the Tuckman stages

It is likely you will have made observations of the group's progress based on a range of evidence including the way the group has operated, your input needed and the degree of achievement and harmony of the group in relation to their agreed goal and learning ground rules. Perhaps recognising each stage of the group's process will allow you as a group worker to be more effective as a member of the group or leader/facilitator. Recognising that a group has necessary stages it will organically pass through also allows for you as group worker to acknowledge each stage and be less anxious of subjective judgements about the group's development and enables you to be vigilant in allowing these stages to happen in a safe environment. It also calls for differing inputs from you as a group facilitator or leader that will be explored in Chapter 6. It's worth noting that there is probably a stage in which you feel most comfortable and so can be aware of areas where you feel less confident and would do well to improve.

Communication

Group workers need to explore their own and others' means of communication in order that they can be conscious about their input and effect on group work dynamics. This would ultimately allow members and facilitators to choose and try out more appropriate responses rather than respond in an unconscious reactive way. Communication in groups can be divided into two sectors, non verbal and verbal. Albert Mehrabian (1971) found that 55 per cent of what we communicate is communicated non verbally, 38 per cent is by our tone and only seven per cent is by our words alone. Most would now agree that words are used for information and that body language is a more powerful 'communicator' than words or tone (Thompson, 1996).

Body language is the main means of conveying messages to others. Non-verbal communication includes;

- facial expression of eyebrows, forehead, mouth;
- eye contact;
- body posture, including arms and legs;
- orientation of body to others – standing and sitting;
- proximity to others in groups or pairs;
- touch;
- fine and gross movements (e.g. by hands, fingers, arms);
- artefacts/dress/setting.

Non-verbal communication composes of over half the content of communication of the sighted community and is much more initially significant than verbal interaction. Non verbal gestures have a link with words in that it can reinforce, modify, substitute and regulate the spoken communication.

Verbal communication includes the tone used and the words chosen.

Tone of voice is the second most important issue followed finally by the words people choose. Tone can include: speed; tone; pitch-intonation; register of formal speech; and loudness. When an individual's body language, tone and words are aligned then their communication is at its most powerful (Thompson, 1996).

It is useful to observe people in social groups you come across in everyday circumstances. In particular people's body language in pubs, cafés and on trains can give you clues about the unspoken conversations they are having and provide you with possible evidence for your assumptions and interpretations. Body language can, for example, be affirming of what is being said or might be confrontational. Different parts of the body continually give clues to our assumptions of the interactions between people. It also gives us insight with our own body language signals which are so important when facilitating group work. Tone of the spoken communication can provide clues about the impact and intention of communications. Once the 'evidence' of the communication has been gathered and assumptions have been drawn, it is wise to explore if there are any other potential alternative interpretations to your 'facts' and observations that could provide a richer reflective account.

Soon you will become more astute at noticing your own and others' body language and tone of voice, and you can become more proactive with your actions rather than reactive. Understanding this skill at a personal level is not so that you can manipulate better but become more aware of ways you can intervene appropriately in an equitable way (see later Thompson's PCS model (2001) re equality). All this is will contribute to you becoming a more effective group member or group work facilitator.

Group roles

The main research around the distinction of roles in groups has focused around enquiries into team work often within businesses. Two key distinctions were defined: 'Task' and 'Maintenance'. Both are fundamental to the balance needed for functioning groups. A group consisting of all high scores of 'task' people may get the job done but the administrative complementary tasks could be left unfinished (such as contracts and budgets) and relationships within the group could be strained and members feel unsupported. There may be no tea and coffee breaks and little work on joint planning, joint tasks and monitoring. However, a group made up of all maintenance people will have very good support structures, have established a high regard for people's feelings and may have good well-documented plans and so on, but little would have been done on the group goals and no one would have led the action or been leading the problem solving and achieving the group goals. A balanced team of task and maintenance people deliver on their aims in a harmonious and supportive way.

Understanding different roles for effective group work has been driven by research in a business context where there is a major concern for promoting effective team working of employees around identified commercial projects. Community and youth group workers have needed to adapt this work to fit their working context routed in social justice values and principles of a practice that enhances informal education, empowerment and community activism.

This was further developed in the 1970s by business researchers such as Dr Meredith Belbin (1993) who experimented within Henley Management College and asserted that any team has nine characters with specific characteristics. He developed a questionnaire that enabled each team member to identify which character they most represented in approach, skills, attitude and style. Others (such as Anthony Jay in the *Observer* 1980) have taken Belbin's concept and continued to create new and helpful distinctions within the nine identified roles. Jay has observed that there needs to be a balance of inward (aligned with task roles) and outward (aligned with maintenance roles) characters to make a group or team effective.

Task people (Belbin roles of chair/co-ordinator, plant, resource investigator and shaper) are natural doers and eager to start achieving the goals. Maintenance people (identified by Belbin's implementer, monitor/evaluator, team worker and finisher) are more interested in building the infrastructure of the group and ensuring that the group's support needs are being met. Obviously these two aspects are both necessary for an effective group and too heavy a reliance on one aspect will skew the group's ability to successfully undertake their group aims and objectives.

Belbin's initial work is still central to group work thinking as many training consultants since the 1980s have continued to develop and create different distinctions of the nine characteristics as model business training and team building.

Questionnaires that can help identify individual Belbin roles can be found on Belbin-related websites. Once you have answered the questionnaire you can then score your answers and from your results identify your scores against the relevant Belbin roles. Your top marks will highlight your strongest characteristics and the role(s) you are more naturally likely to play in a group. Your lowest score will point to the most unlikely role you should undertake and maybe the group role you appreciate the least. Once you have this understanding of your strongest role then you can take steps to improve consciously and conscientiously your skills and responses in groups so that you can enhance the way you play this role and appreciate other roles as well as improve on your weaker characteristics.

For those of us not in business employment, we need to ensure that the application of Belbin's interpretation of team working is placed in an appropriate empowering and equitable framework of group work especially on project and self-directed group work. Understanding power and how it can be harnessed to become an empowering tool is critical for any informal educator involved in group work practice.

Power leadership and inclusion

If we do not take account of social factors such as sexism, racism, ageism and disablism, we will be able to do justice to only those individuals who are fortunate not to be subject to any form of oppression. For those who do experience oppression, we shall be ill-equipped to respond appropriately to the reality of their experience, and will therefore run the risk of actually adding to their oppression.

We can conclude, then, that all practice needs to be anti-discriminatory practice, in so far as approaches that are not sensitive to discrimination will not only miss significant aspects of the situation, but may actually do a great deal of harm.

(Thompson, 1996, p162)

Power and leadership are key factors that can affect the ability of a group to be an empowered and enlightened experience. There are three key factors to consider that affect the functions of groups (adapted from Gibson and Clarke 1995) and ultimately its ability to include all:

1 focus i.e. the aims of the group;

2 inter-group communication, including the group's decision-making process;

3 relationships within the group, e.g. roles and norms.

Communication is fundamental to the delivery of inclusive and enlightened interactions; as mentioned before, any dialogue is linked to values and beliefs. It is a complex process that involves both those who are verbally interacting and those who are actively listening. It can involve a strong link to members' identity and who they think they are. It shapes conversations and is open to interpretation and reinterpretation by others. Empowering communication is a major part of the underlying principles of community and youth workers' practice. A group worker therefore needs to identify an aligned leadership style with similar empowering principles.

The group worker needs to approach leadership as a means to allow for the maximum of participation by each member. At times this may mean being facilitative and at other occasions being directive. Whichever approach is chosen, it has to be in response to what is decided as necessary for maximum empowerment. Any empowering leadership skills are likely to benefit from the facilitator being accountable and transparent about their power, intentions and commitment to the group.

To maximise an empowering facilitative approach, it would be necessary to examine each of the three factors of focus, communication and relationships to identify ways that could then increase ownership and collective identity. For example, working on the aims of the group, and after agreeing the principles for a group learning environment, a worker could then facilitate a way that the whole group can collectively set their group aims that are agreed and clearly understood. The group facilitator can enhance the group communication by checking that the group has a 'listening ear' for the positive contribution possible by each member and that not one person's opinion or ideas dominate. Group dynamics must allow for members to hold their own values and be fluid in their roles and responsibilities appropriate to the occasions.

The membership of most secondary groups often needs to be revisited and enhanced so that it can be as inclusive as possible (Mullender and Ward 1991). If the group is constructed around an issue then it needs to be widely advertised. As there is often no formal selection process, group members who are in discriminated communities, for example black and/or women members, need to be given clear 'signals' that they are welcome to join and reassured that any racist or sexist behaviour won't be tolerated. Ideally, this is established in the learning agreements at the outset and the group kept aligned to these 'rules' by the group membership.

CASE STUDY

Group work ownership and participation

You are a local area youth worker, attached to the council, and have been at the first of many area consultation meetings at the local community centre attended by local residents, including a handful of local young people (all males aged mainly 13 to 14 years old), about what the residents want from the regeneration scheme. These lads got kicked out for messing about with the papers and the model brought along by the council, so you followed them outside and chatted to them about the incident and what they thought about their area. They complained about nothing to do and poor local play areas where disgruntled residents complained if they even sat on the swings. They didn't want to return inside and went off to the local shops.

A week later, the council lets you know there is money for a small-scale project for a play area in the nearby park.

When exploring this scenario you need to have thought through your style of intervention with the group. Would a formal approach suit the group or an informal approach? What preparation would you need to do before talking to them?

You already have some understood power over them as the recognised youth leader in terms of age and status and you need to acknowledge this and be clear what your boundaries in regard to this project are. If they are willing to form a group to look at developing a new play project, then you need to establish a learning contract with them. You could also then explore with the group similar issues such as membership, boundaries and agreed aims and embark on facilitating the group through the Tuckman's stages.

In the membership debate it is your role to make sure they explore the limitations of a single-gender group and possible single age, ethnicity, sexuality and ability group on the kind of aims and plans for the play area. You need to begin to think about ways you could help the group identify ways they could find of approaching and including others' opinions i.e. those of young women, younger and older people, lesbian and gay people, people with special needs who may live in the area.

Your role will be to also find workable communication means between the Council meetings and this group in the long term which could include suggesting to the group that they work on presentation skills and communication awareness. Ultimately you need to use tools (e.g. Mullender and Ward's model) to move your ownership of the project into their control and leadership.

Leadership and change

Group workers have at their disposal a variety of group work leadership styles that perform certain functions to enhance the group process. It is useful if the group facilitator/leader is aware of their own style and range of available approaches and their consequences.

The Lewin et al. (1939) model of leadership includes four types that have been adapted here to match community and youth work context.

1 Authoritative (makes the decisions, sets the parameters of the agenda and keeps the group on tasks, provides most of input, directs the tasks).

2 Consultative (creates a system where, as a leader, they can hold a final veto, keeps the group to learning agreements).

3 Enabling (enables decisions to be made collectively, supportive).

4 Laissez-faire (allows the group to be responsible for clarifying, no input as a leader unless invited, acts more like an equal member than facilitator).

There will be times in a group's cycle when one or the other style will be more appropriate than another although there is probably a preferred natural style that each group finds the most comfortable.

ACTIVITY **5.5**

Consider leadership styles. Can you identify what style you think you naturally fall into for the following:

* *Within primary groups such as family and friends.*

* *Within work in a group on the street.*

* *With a peer staff group such as your area workers' meetings.*

* *With young people in activity-orientated objectives.*

* *What style would you welcome further training in developing the necessary skills? What would be those skills?*

There are no clear answers to these questions as differing circumstances will require different approaches. What you need to be able to do as a group worker is to adapt to the style that is needed, rather than react in unconscious and uncontrolled ways. Inability to move out of a particular type would be an inhibiting experience for group members and could be an inappropriate response. Some people find they are more able to be assertive and clear and engaged when they are in a task role, i.e. as facilitator, chair or worker. For others issues such as gender, race, age and other communities of identity power dynamics affect group participation and use of leadership skills.

Empowerment and group work for social change

Mullender and Ward (1991) have outlined a useful model of self-directed group work. Their model has identifiable key stages to enable and create empowering group relationships and communication. These stages are explained in more detail later on in this section and can be aligned within Tuckman's (1965) five stages of group work process. Here are a few examples of the key skills needed for each stage.

- Forming stage needs great organisational skills and ability to put people at their ease.

- Storming stage needs to be comfortable and requires adept skills at handing conflict.

- Norming stage needs skills in summarising and keeping everyone included and organised into action.

- Performing stage needs an ability to take a back seat and be supportive, and to provide links for people to undertake the tasks.

- Mourning stage needs skills in being good at acknowledging people's contributions, ability in ending evaluations, giving constructive feedback and letting go of past upsets.

Mullender and Ward's (1991) self-directed group work model looks at appropriate group work leadership within a community activist practice model and imposes three key questions: What? Why? How? These questions can be superimposed into the appropriate stage of Tuckman's model (see Figure 5.1) so as to support a group work model designed for users' self-direction and empowerment. For example: in the initial stage of forming, in the Mullender and Ward model, the worker encourages the group to take stock; in the storming and norming stage, the group members continue to 'take stock' and begin to 'take off'.

In the norming stage the group workers encourage the members to clarify 'what' are the problems/issues being tackled. The group workers then encourage the group to focus on the wider context of the chosen group issue and explore 'why' the issue exists. This is then followed by asking 'how' the group can produce the change they require.

At the performing stage, the group 'takes off' and starts to 'take over'.

At Tuckman's ending stage, after the group has taken over and completed their task the facilitator asks the group to revisit and reformulate again the three key questions in the ending stage by reviewing the what, the why and the how.

This then completes the ownership/take over of the group members with the process having far-reaching self-esteem results for both the individual and the group.

Figure 5.2 illustrates the two models and begins to capture a range of group facilitators' leadership skills at each stage.

ACTIVITY 5.6

Imagine you are a group facilitator. Ask yourself this question:

- *What are the pros and cons of Lewin's four adapted leadership styles of authoritative/ consultative/enabling/laissez-faire for each of Tuckman's five stages of forming/storming/ norming/performing/mourning?*

Tuckman model	Mullender and Ward model	Facilitator style
Forming	Taking stock.	Directive. Enabling. Setting up learning environment for safety.
Storming	Taking stock.	Directive and enabling. Calm and safe to allow for conflict. Holder of original aims.
Norming	Taking off.	Empowering and constructive feedback. Enabling decision-making. Flexibility and monitoring ability to revisit roles and responsibilities. Asking: • What? • Why • How?
Performing	Taking off. Taking over.	Supportive. Resourcing the action. Reminder of inclusivity.
Mourning/ending		Enable emotional acknowledgement. Evaluation as ending process. Ability to let go. Revisiting: • What? • Why? • How?

Figure 5.2 The Tuckman model and Mullender and Ward model: capturing a range of group facilitators' leadership skills at each stage

Now you have explored a range of styles appropriate for each stage that could achieve the same outcome. However, there are parts of the four styles that lend themselves to the following stages.

Stages	Leadership styles
Forming	Authorative/Enabling
Storming	Consultative/Enabling
Norming	Enabling/Authorative
Performing	Laissez-faire/Enabling
Mourning	Enabling/Authorative

Figure 5.3 Tuckman's stages and their leadership styles

There is a balance to be struck between the different styles, for example being so authoritative that the group never has the opportunity to become self-directed and motivated and being so laissez-faire that the group loses focus and direction. The best results are probably achieved by having an ability to reflect in the action (see Schön 1983, 1991 in the chapter on reflection and enquiry) and to be able to draw on a range of styles as and when deemed necessary from your reflective assessments.

Preston-Shoot (2007) examined the five Tuckman's stages and noticed that in some groups the first three stages of forming, storming and norming can happen in a different order if the group truly tackles the issue of inclusion and diversity for all its group members. It's possible that a group coming through the storming and norming process that has not taken the opportunity to explore prejudicial opinions and values in any depth may collude, maybe unknowingly, with discriminatory values and beliefs. This can then result in a group re-storming after norming when an issue of exclusion presents itself.

For example, a group of workers taking part in staff training had been working together for six weeks on a variety of in service issues for a NVQ in Youth Work. This week they were exploring equality and had been exploring a scenario of an issue of racism set in a youth club setting. The group consisted of six adults: three white men, two white women and one black woman.

The five white workers look to the one black woman for the 'right' answer and generally feel uncomfortable expressing their own opinions. In the previous session one of the men had noticed how the black woman had been 'taken away' from the key debate about resources, by being allocated the role of the observer and given little choice to say no. He wanted to raise this matter as he felt uncomfortable when it happened the previous week but had said nothing and was clear that he had colluded with this act of racism. He was now feeling even more uncomfortable with the current situation of the other group members singling the black woman out as the 'other' and took the chance to say as he felt. This caused some of the white male and female group members to become angry and challenge him, accusing him of sabotaging the group from completing their task within the deadline of the allocated time on an insignificant point.

The group, after a few hot exchanges, renegotiated the task with the overall facilitators and continued to explore all their feelings and went back to re-forming and re-norming as a group. They all said it was a valuable learning process that had taken them out of a cosy comfortable place and how valuable the process had been.

Group work can and should provide a vehicle for practice to explore and challenge values and beliefs and it needs to develop critical thinking within its membership.

ACTIVITY 5.7

Think of an issue in community and youth work you are passionate to alter for the better.

- *Ask yourself 'What?', then 'Why?', then 'How?'*

- *Write down your key points and consider how you could work with a group of similarly passionate people wanting the same change. What would be your strong point as a group leader?*

Solution-focused group work practice and leadership

Group work within community and youth work practice has adapted and developed a variety of approaches and tools from therapeutic group work practitioners, especially since the 1960s. Solution-focused (SF) practice has a set of principles and tools adapted for group work practices. (Please also refer to Chapter 6 for a more detailed account of SF practice for tools and methods that are useful in one-to-one encounters as well as with groups.) This approach was created by therapists in America who have developed creative ways of becoming more 'group member' centred. The SF practice has a similar set of empowering principles that complement effective empowering group work practices – that is, they found it important that they:

- work with the person rather than the problem;
- look for resources rather than deficits;
- explore possible and preferred futures;
- explore what is currently working;
- treat people as the experts in their own lives (adapted from Sharry, 2001).

Solution-focused work is underpinned by these sets of beliefs and principles and has sets of tools and approaches that Sharry explores in his account of SF group work practice. He identifies a set of aims especially for SF group work that include the need to focus on change, the need to identify clear goals and preferred futures and work that builds on strengths, skills and resources. His group work practice uses a solution framework for solving problems through what he calls 'problem-free' talk. The practice starts from a positive perspective by identifying the items that are working and encourages group practioners to continue to develop and enhance these practices rather than highlighting problems or unworkable areas. For SF group work to operate, it needs to exist within a context of respectful curiosity, and create a co-operative and collaborative group working environment. It does not ignore the fact that certain dynamics within groups can be inhibited by the uncooperative stance of individual group members and collective group members (Sharry, 2001 and Preston-Shoot, 2007). Chapter 6 will explore the issue of applying solution-focused practice and methods to group work and in particular to a range of people who display difficult behaviour.

Understanding equality

Every interaction with people is inherently influenced by the dynamics of gender, race, sexuality, age, religious context, class, abilities, etc. These distinctions have to be explicitly dealt with in all effective group dynamics. A group worker needs to be aware of their own personal prejudice, cultural discrimination and structural dilemmas (Thompson, 2001 and Mullender and Ward, 1991).

Your group work is informed by your individual professional practice which is informed by two main aspects of everyone's own professional knowledge.

First, by the worker's organisational knowledge learned from internal professional training and personal development once involved in voluntary or paid professional youth and community work in their working environment. Second and equally important is the aspect of the workers' individual knowledge achieved from inherent values, beliefs and experiences gathered from family, siblings, friends, school culture and leisure environment, etc. It involves interactions with significant others – also called experiential, situated (Lave and Wenger, 1991) or active (owned) and understood (Hedegaard 1988).

Professional knowledge impacts upon practice and is influenced by many internal and external factors and is worth investigating especially in relationship to equality issues. As workers we need to understand our own professional knowledge so we can be conscious about its strengths and limitations when operating within a group work environment that is influenced by all of the group members' own values and experiences, so the group works within a context that is as equitable as possible.

RESEARCH ACTIVITY

Identify a recent group interaction or situation in your work. Detail the interaction.

- *Critically review the situation or intervention in regard to two aspects of professional knowledge.*

- *What decisions did you make and why?*

- *What informed those decisions to intervene in the way that you did in regard to your professional knowledge?*

- *Where did this information/knowledge stem from?*

- *Can you identify any gaps in your own knowledge base?*

- *How has your practice evolved through experience?*

- *What has significantly contributed to your professional maturation?*

- *How do you relate to your initial training? What have you modified, adapted, developed in the course of your work and study?*

- *What theory knowledge and skills do you base your group work practice upon?*

- *How do you/will you bring this experience and knowledge into your professional group work facilitator role?*

- *What skills, knowledge and attitudes do you feel are important in the delivery of your community and youth group work?*

You will find that your current professional knowledge has been acquired from significant past experiences and conversations in schooling, with peers, family and friends. Parts of this knowledge could be untested and powerful in how it informs your practice today. Other sources of information you will have gathered while training in your profession and you will need to be aware of the links to theory and practice evidence. All group workers will also have absorbed inherited outdated prejudicial assumptions and need to be vigilant to address these areas of ignorance that could then result in unintentional discriminatory practices. This commitment to your re-education, coupled with a willingness to challenge your's and others' untested personal assumptions are necessary group work skills and attitudes that will promote equality and inclusion.

Personal understanding and the impact it has upon equality and the empowering process is one of three key distinctions of the equality model as defined by Thompson's PCS model (2001). He describes three layers that are intertwined and in which the dynamic of power and oppression operate. The layers relate to the personal or prejudicial (P level), the community or cultural level (C level) and the structural or societal layers (S level).

The personal level represents the individual prejudicial aspect of oppression and equality. Personalised awareness training programmes have been conducted extensively since the 1980s addressing workers' thoughts and assumed stereotypes that promote oppressive practice. Training programmes focused on changing personal prejudicial attitudes have run alongside the emergence of each of the community movements especially in the 1970s and 1980s. This progress in increasing personal awareness is an ongoing process as power and oppression is deeply rooted.

The cultural level is sandwiched in-between the P and S levels and has been the main operating area for youth and communities to effect change. It is in this arena that workers have worked with groups in effective campaigning project work to create significant changes in their local communities. These grass roots groups and grass root group workers have operated within the C level with probably less obvious model strategies and successes than the P and S levels because of its disparate and dynamic nature.

Within the 'S' or structural level the community and youth sector operated within an intensive worldwide set of community equality activists' movements of the black and women's communities from the 1960s to 1980s. It provided an era of personal awareness training that challenged the prejudicial and stereotyping thoughts and actions of those involved in people services. Alongside this, the UK government began to introduce in the 1970s an infrastructure of acts and legislations around equality issues starting with race and gender, to enforce good practice and policy within mainly public bodies and provide a legal framework for individuals to challenge prejudicial behaviour.

Gender and equality has been an issue taken up by community and youth workers within their communities, especially concerned with the vibrant energy of the women's movement and feminism driving the 1980s working with girls and young women. This enhanced the group work undertaken with women- and girls-only members, often in activist campaigning group work with an aim of developing an awareness of the effects of sexism and the way to challenge women's rights and uncover and protect female values and approaches (Cohen and Mullender, 2003).

There is an abundance of resources and information available for groups to stimulate the debate and discussions around understanding and developing consciousness around sexism. It is empowering group work practice to work with the groups' agenda wherever possible. As a group worker facilitator it is also sensible to be prepared to take opportunities to be proactive in raising the issues of power and discrimination by having a range of useful resources available.

The following resource could extend the group debate from the personal to the structural through examining the cultural experiences worldwide and relating this back to individual members' understanding of their experiences and professional knowledge.

For example, read the following statement taken from PLAN UK, a London-based charity who launched a worldwide campaign with their recent report 'Because I am a Girl' in September 2009.

> *There is evidence that by the age of 5 both girls and boys have already internalised their gender roles that are expected to play – and the status that these roles will or will not give them. Therefore the influence during this initial stage really does shape their attitudes.*

(PLAN UK Report 'Because I am a Girl', 2009, p189)

You could use this to stimulate discussion with a group of mixed or single gender membership who are open to looking at discrimination and exploring their place within discrimination and their own personal experiences of childhood and gender and where these messages came from, who reinforced them, etc. It is possible to then take the debate wider into the societal sphere by introducing (from the same report 2009) these structural issues regarding gender:

- *25% of the world population are girls and young women;*
- *62% of illiterate young people are young women;*
- *70,000 10-year-old girls are married;*
- *14 million under 18 year olds are mothers;*
- *66% of 15–19 year olds with HIV are female;*
- *50% of sexual assaults are against girls.*

These figures could then trigger a debate about the implications of the worldview of young women and the impact of issues such as education, health and children's rights in relation to young women and girls' discrimination.

Evaluation and review

Reviewing a group process needs to happen throughout all the different sessions and stages and be brought together at the final stage. A review left only at the end of a group will lack detail and depth and often miss the journey undertaken by the group and only recall the significant features as remembered in the group's last stage. It is therefore important that there is an understanding of what is going to be reviewed and the methods of evaluation to be initiated from the start. Parts of the group journey will be easier to review than others. There are group work items that are quantifiable and can be counted which include items such as attendance, number of objectives achieved, etc. However, other issues such as concepts, principles, values, dynamics that underpin effective group work are quality issues and do not lend themselves to easy ways of assessment.

It is suggested that there are eight key necessary qualitative aspects inherent in effective groups worthy of reviewing:

- good respectful relationships;

- ability for collaborative, inclusive, co-operative action;

- clear, agreed, transparent aims;

- individual accountability and self-generated responsibility;

- ability to make collective decisions;

- ability to empower and create change;

- effective communication;

- clear, valued, understood roles.

(adapted from Gibson and Clark, 1995, p40).

Evaluation has its derivative in the Latin and means 'strength' and 'empower'. It has strayed from this original intention and today is often about proving something is working or needed and/or improving practice sometimes within a context of a set of externally imposed criteria. However, the original meaning of strength and power is especially useful to remember for community and youthworkers' practice.

The purpose of evaluation is to reflect critically on the effectiveness of personal and professional practice. It is to contribute to the development of 'good' rather than 'correct' practice (Everitt and Hardiker, 1996, p129). So what do we use to reflect on 'good' group work practice? This infers it's more than counting and measuring. What models are in youth and community practice we can draw upon for group work evaluation?

There are many forms/models of evaluation though they all have in common a means of valuing the practice. How the value is measured and judged varies depending on differing circumstances. This creates different distinctions of evaluating that is applied in group work evaluation thinking.

There are also different ways of measuring any overall group achievements and individual session outputs or goals:

- Quantitative

  - Counting

  - Ticking boxes

- Qualitative

  - Personal accounts

  - Scaling questions

  - Drawings, etc.

Group qualitative evaluations can and do use a variety of tools for 'measurements' such as members' case studies of their involvement in their group progress, reflective diaries, oral accounts taped or videoed and photographs. Groups could use their skills or draw on skills from other disciplines such as in craft (e.g. knitting, drawing and painting, flower work,

107

woodwork), in sport (e.g. gymnastics), in drama and literature (e.g. role play, scenarios, reviews, etc.).

The following contains the key elements in two categories: external focused process and value base, and internal focused process and value base.

Qualitative	Quantitative
Dialogue	Banking
Practice	Programme + Project
Formative	Summative
Internal	External

Figure 5.4 The key elements of external focused process and value base, and internal focused process and value base (adapted from Robson, 1993 and Smith, 2001)

The external approach of evaluation or banking model (Smith) can be adapted to the exploration of group work evaluations. It is process driven and uses values and objective quantitative indicators that are generated from the concept of a 'neutral expert's' programme evaluation based on 'counting' items. This quantitative model is inherited from a business laden environment with hidden 'conservative' laden values and judgements. This model has its historical routes in the business sector but has its limitations when exploring equality issues within a dynamic of youth and community practice and especially in group work practices.

The internal approach or Dialogical (Smith) or Formative approach (Robson) model is based on a qualitative approach to evaluations. In group work it is an evaluation style that assesses and monitors quality activities such as conversations, negotiations and degree of group consensus, etc. This approach allows for subjective practice approaches. It is underpinned by empowerment principles adapted from the understanding of Foucault (see Chapter 4) and Freire's (1972) theories of power, collective action and participation.

The overall context of evaluation of community and youth group work will benefit from a dialogue approach as this allows for capturing the flexible dynamic nature of group work and equality values and beliefs.

The next section will consider in more detail ways and concepts that are appropriate in exploring evaluation for group work in answering three key questions; 'why' evaluate?; 'what' to evaluate?; and 'how' to evaluate?

Why evaluate?

After being clear about the overall evaluative context, as workers we then need to focus in on why we are evaluating the group. There are five reasons for asking 'why?'

1 To provide evidence for progress.

2 To learn from what works in practice.

3 To learn from what doesn't work in practice.

4 To identify change in practice.

5 To improve your and the group's effectiveness.

Evaluation is a measurement of some kind and for it to be as empowering and effective as possible within community and youth context it has be creative and dynamic enough to include empowerment and equality. The Dialogue qualitative model lends itself to this approach.

After identifying 'why', it is necessary to identify 'what', then to identify 'how' to measure such concepts as equality, empowerment, etc.

What to evaluate?

Any group work needs at the outset to have identified what the group is doing and from this, devise a means of evaluating what is going to be measured. It is also useful to think about both the internal and external measurements.

Internal factors have been explored by most aligned people services that use group work in their professions and involve evaluating individual development and gained individual skills, plus the groups' progress and skill development overall. Mullender and Ward (1991) also identify external issues that are important for community and youth workers whose approach is equally routed in collective change and activism and who recognise the need to capture a separate set of external factors 'measured' by others outside the group such as the improvement of other community agencies' opinions of the group, the consequent development of community services, etc.

Ledwith (**www.infed.org/group work/what_is_a_group.htm**) has identified a useful selection of group measurements:

- group interaction – task and relationships;

- group interdependence – social networks;

- group structure – size, norms and roles;

- group goals – co-operative and competitive;

- group cohesion and something Ledwith called 'groupness'.

Group cohesion or 'entitativity' is the measurement of the degree of 'groupness' or sameness between members of a group. Clues come from how they communicate/similar behaviours/ dress codes/and proximity (seen in primary groups and developed in secondary groups).This group identity is clearly seen in young people's groups, for example Goths, Emos, etc. According to Preston-Shoot (2007), groups need to be responsive and flexible, working in an inclusive and involving manner. He notes that there are few available written accounts of group work methodologies or research and while this may allow workers to be creative, they will then have to be clear about their process when under scrutiny.

Looking at Ledwith's suggestions there are some indicators that are potentially quantitative in nature. The challenge for the group worker and its members is to also find creative and imaginative ways to capture the qualitative factors that are central to empowerment and change, as outlined earlier in this chapter.

How to evaluate?

Deciding what to measure needs to be informed by what it is you want to achieve and what the group work focus is.

The following outlines five main areas aligned with Smith's (**www.infed.org/biblio/b-eval. htm**) dialogue model of evaluation and are adapted for the application of measuring group work.

1 Gathering information as process.

2 Monitoring progress.

3 Making good judgements.

4 Exploring and judging.

5 Creating a dialogue with those involved.

Smith argues that these characteristics are aligned with the core practices of effective community and youth work. If the core practice is routed in the art of informal education, the evaluation process needs to reflect this by making collective assessments based on and engaging in conversations and raising questions, considering answers and developing responses.

The tools available to gather information, monitor, explore and create dialogue need to be dynamic and creative appropriate to the essence of good practice.

Using the tool of self-assessment has been a recent innovation introduced within the statutory Local Authorities' evaluations of project and service reviews and is seen as progressive and as working towards empowerment and involvement. However, Smart (2007) debates if the current development of using self-assessment as a tool by community and youth workers really is an empowerment process or another more subtle form of management control.

When deciding how to measure, Preston-Shoot (2007) suggests testing out the following questions in regard to your measurement.

• Is it feasible?

• Is it reliable?

• Is it realistic?

• Is it valid?

Sharry (2001) would support a use of solution-focused reflections on the group's progress and if the group is 'working' don't fix it but identify what is working and do more of the same.

There are therefore a variety of creative means of measuring that are aligned with maximum participation and empowerment principles.

ACTIVITY 5.8

Think of a group you have worked successfully with over the last year.

- *How did you evaluate their progress?*

- *Did you measure them against your bigger aims and objectives?*

- *How did you ensure that key group issues such as equality, social justice and empowerment were evaluated effectively?*

- *Who evaluated?*

- *What one thing are you most proud about in the group's achievement?*

- *If you did it all again what would you change about the evaluation?*

In reflecting on your group work practice you may expose ways of working differently and it could generate new lateral links to your work practice. The understanding of and skills for group work lend themselves to the inclusion of evaluation as part of its process and it is a missed opportunity if seen as a chore to be completed swiftly at the end of a planned event.

C H A P T E R   R E V I E W

This chapter has explored the understanding of which concepts, principles, values and dynamics underpin effective group work within any aligned community and young people work. It has drawn on the relevant social and psychodynamic field from the boom in group working in the 1960s onwards and in particular of those theorists who have developed their work within the people, commercial, formal educational, social and health services.

This has included researchers in the 1960s and 1970s, some connected to the business world (Belbin, 1981, 1993), some to psychological practices (Tuckman, 1965, 1984) and some to early youth work training (Button, 1974). It has drawn on youth practitioners such as Gibson and Clarke's (1995) work on 'Project' group work and social/community group work, for example Mullender's and Ward's (1991) self-directed group work. More recently, there have been developments in relation to a more empowering approach with authors committed to empowering methodology such as Smith (2001) in his exploration of dialogical approaches, Sharry (2001) in his incorporation of solution-focused approaches and Preston-Shoot (2007) who grounds his exploration of group dynamics within social justice and social work settings. Thompson's (2001) PCS model has provided an interesting platform for exploring group work and issues of equality and power.

Effective group work has a major positive educative influence on people's lives and the ability to accredit change in themselves, in their community and in society.

The effect of self-directed groups which run their course through to maturity is both deep and far reaching. On meeting people who have belonged to such groups, it is clear what an impact their involvement has made. It provided a framework for understanding, and experience and skills for handling, the personal and wider relationships of the society in which they are living, even in the face of unemployment, poverty, racism and the other evils of contemporary society.

(Mullender and Ward, 1991, p138)

Effective group work that supports the formation and maintenance of social groups remains an important professional community and youth work intervention. It provides a potential for education, a 'laboratory of democracy' (Knowles, 1994, p111), for informal learning. Groups and group work can provide collective understanding and solutions for change providing informed and committed action – praxis.

FURTHER READING

I would advise anyone looking for more contextual background to group work and equality to read:

Mullender, A and Ward, D (1991) *Self-directed groupwork: users take action for empowerment*. London: Whiting and Birch.

and

Preston-Shoot, M (2007) *Effective groupwork*. Basingstoke: Palgrave Macmillan.

For more hands-on information on skills and understanding for project group work then I suggest:

Gibson, A and Clarke, G (1995) *Project based group work facilitator's manual: young people, youth workers and projects*. London: Jessica Kingsley.

For a good basic overview read Mark Smith's article on what is group work accessed from his infed web site www.infed.org/groupwork/what_is_a_group.htm

If you want to also explore new positive approaches then Sharry (2001) explains the application of solution-focused approaches and methods to group work.

Sharry, J (2001) *Solution-focused group work* (Brief Therapy Series). London: Sage.

Chapter 6
Reflection and enquiry

Frankie Williams

CHAPTER OBJECTIVES

This chapter will help you meet the following National Occupational Standards.

1.2.4 Support young people in evaluating the impact of youth work upon their own development

4.2.3 Identify and address new youth work opportunities

5.1.1 Work as an effective and reflective practitioner

5.1.2 Manage your own resources and professional development

5.3.1 Provide support to other workers

5.3.2 Provide learning opportunities for colleagues

It will also introduce you to the following academic standards as set out in the youth and community work benchmark statement. (2009, QAA)

7.1
• Recognise and compare multiple, competing perspectives and challenge the status quo and dominant perspectives.
• Question and be prepared to deconstruct taken for granted and common sense professional understandings.

7.2
• Operate as critical and reflective practitioners.
• Promote experiential learning and reflection in self and others.

Introduction

Reflective practice is at the heart of creative work with people. Community and youth work settings have historically encouraged workers to include regular reflective practices within their professional staff development and professional training courses at all levels involving workers in reflection work either on their own, within peer groups and/or with tutors.

It could be argued that reflection involves the process of unlearning and unpacking our subconscious thoughts and actions by a form of guided enquiry. The term 'reflection' comes from a Latin derivative that means to bend backwards and forwards (Smith, **www.infed. org/evaluation**). This is useful to apply to reflective practice as it aids and elucidates the process of an effective enquiry that goes in two directions: it applies our critical thinking to what we have done, and then relates this learning to inform our future reflections and actions.

Questions as reflection cues are key in reflective practices. As we discussed in Chapter 1, asking questions is the basis for generating theory and extending our horizons of understanding. They are also at the centre of the tools used in reflective frameworks of our own thoughts and models, especially within the model of appreciative enquiry explored in more detail later. This model highlights how a different construction of questioning and approach can purposefully dictate the type and context of the answers we receive. Different models provide differing questioning that can aid the reflection and analysis of experiences with the intention of improving work-based practices.

The kinds of questions we ask are at the heart of the process and can evoke different aspects of the work. For example the question 'How do I do it?' provokes an enquiry into an analytical reflection of the worker's action or observations. The evaluative reflective question 'How well did I do it?' provokes investigation that allows for evaluations after the event and is sometimes referred to as reflection-on-action.

This chapter will explore the nature of reflection and its place in professional practice. First, it will explore some of the main theoretical perspectives behind different forms of reflection and look at a sample of the tools we can employ to help with reflective processes. The second main strand of this chapter will then examine reflection-on-action and the role of supervision and in particular solution-focused supervision using the appreciative enquiry model. In the context of community and youth work this model is particularly appropriate as it provides a framework for an empowerment process in both the relationship between reflector and supervisor and helps to develop a learning model that empowers workers in their practice.

Reflective practice and theory

Looking at a theoretical base for reflective practice two key 1980s thinkers have inspired models and ways of looking at reflective and critical learning in informal education and solution-focused appreciative enquiry. Schön (1983) and Kolb (1984) have developed ways of describing the reflective process in professional practices, though as Cowan (1998) points out they do this for different purposes. Kolb's cycle describes a process of reflection and action starting with the point of an experience that is then reflected on to create a more general concept or idea of what had occurred that can then be put into a new action. The cycle is devised as a means of exploration and action stages that help the worker to examine a piece of work that has an identified goal or outcome. Schön requires the reflector to step back while in action giving the chance for a variety of reflective snapshots of their practice.

The next section will now explore in more depth the two reflective thinkers' ideas.

Schön

Schön investigated the use of reflective supervision support and was concerned with the process and quality of the decision-making process of individual professionals. He believed that professional workers did what worked without a great deal of conscious thought to how and why it worked for them. He termed this unconscious routine as knowing-in-action or reflection-in-action. Workers with people often say they work instinctively in situations and when questioned later, they can't always articulate what they know works. They are clear that it does work but they don't know why.

This form of reflection is sometimes referred to as thinking on your feet. Workers will recognise this process as it's a familiar everyday way they operate in their face to face work. Practitioners often find themselves in differing and perhaps untested, unexpected new situations in which quick decisions about how to act need to be made. In this process workers make use of a wide range of different tools, which include using their intuition, established techniques and practice skills. As Smith points out the ability to improvise and be creative, rather than following a set routine is what makes a worker 'special'. However, the relative time restriction in which decisions need to be made means that we cannot always think things through thoroughly and our thinking might be incomplete (Smith, 1994, p129).

As a result, reflection needs to be revisited after the event when a different range of thoughts and feelings can be addressed.

> *Practitioners do reflect on their knowing-in-practice. Sometimes in the relative tranquillity of a post-mortem, they think back on a project they have undertaken, a situation they have lived through, and they explore the understanding they have brought to the handling of the case. They may do this in a mood of idle speculation, or in a deliberate effort to prepare themselves for future cases.*
>
> (Schön, 1983, p61)

Schön gave value to this approach and identified a further distinction of creating reflection after the event, a term he coined 'knowledge-on-action' or reflection-on-action (1983, p54) that then occurs once the worker reflects on their knowledge-in-action or reflection-in-action. He promoted professional supervision as a valuable space for this reflection and explored the same and different tools and approaches for two different professions. Today as an enhancement of the quality of professional practice, supervision is still at the heart of learning organisations' practice. It is practised regularly and provides boundaried support for professional workers where they are encouraged to reflect on and try to make sense of their work or 'reflection-in-action' and turn it into 'reflection-on-action'. This will then provide the basis for informing their future undertakings and will be of benefit in their individual professional practice, for their agency and ultimately for everyone they work with.

Many authors later built on Schön's work and developed further distinctions. As well as the stages of reflection in and on action, Boud, Keogh and Walker (1985) recognised the need for pre-action experience, something Cowan (1998, pp36, 38) called reflection for action.

We will continue to explore reflection for, in and on action later in this chapter.

Kolb

Kolb (1984) was also developing a reflective model about the same time as the major work of Boud, Keogh and Walker (1985). He devised an action learning model to capture how to dissect the process of learning from experience. This concept originated from the thinking of Lewin (1952) and has been a stable feature for teaching and learning of informal and formal education. Kolb's cyclical model involves four stages: experience; reflection; generalisation; and testing.

Starting with a direct experience (that will include reflection-in-action), we are encouraged to reflect on (reflection-on-action) what we think has happened and why. At the next stage we are then asked to generalise from our initial reflection, i.e. we can think about what we have learned so far. This might involve an element of abstraction where we think about how our learning could be applied more generally and to different circumstances. This allows us to search for different ways of doing things by using our initial reflections to inform how our learning is affecting our practice. Finally we can experiment a little with our new found clarity and test a new approach (taking action from our reflection-on-action). This new approach then provides another experience from which we can start the process of reflection all over again.

The next activity is designed to explore how the cycle could work in a student or worker common activity and will give you the opportunity to think through the stages with a potentially familiar situation. It also provides you with a chance to practise reflection-on-action.

ACTIVITY **6.1**

Look back at an assignment or report you have written for work that you submitted, that was not as good as it could have been.

- *Did you receive feedback from others on your work?*

- *What did the feedback for the assignment/report tell you – what were its strengths and what has been suggested you could do differently?*

- *What do you think would have helped you make this a better piece of work?*

- *What have you learned from this?*

- *What are your explanations?*

- *Do your reflections tell you something a bit more generally than just relating to this piece of work? For example, looking at time management and contextual issues – did you run out of time and therefore had to rush some sections?*

- *Why was this – did you start too late? Were there a lot of other deadlines coming together?*

- *Were you unclear about what you were actually asked to do?*

- *Is it difficult for you to find a quiet space to work at work or home? Do you study alongside your work and there are just not enough hours in the week? Did you just experience unforeseen events in your family life or other areas of work?*

- *What could you do differently next time? Could you ask for support before completing the work – for example, ask for a session with your supervisor or tutor to make sure you are on the right track? Arrange to work in a group with some of your peers? Make a flowchart to see when deadlines are coming up?*

- *Think long and hard about the balance between your paid work and study and make some adjustments. Who else can you ask for support? What kind of support do you need? Could you ask for an extension of the deadline? Could you improve where you write, i.e. could you work in the library, in your office or someone else's quiet work space?*

- *Make some decisions about what you are actually going to do differently and see how it goes – and then of course start this process again. What worked well? Which bits did not? Is there any fine-tuning required?*

From this exercise and the previous Schön model, you will now be becoming familiar with reflection-on-action as well as Kolb's cycle of learning that has reflection at the heart of the process. The following section explores further tools and models that will aid your ability to be a reflective thinker.

Reflective recordings

The next section explores reflective accounts and diaries as a tool for capturing thoughts from reflection-in-action and can build this enquiry to explore reflections-on-action (as examined in the last section). Reflection-on-action comes as a later process allowing time and distance from the original experience of thinking on your feet aided by recordings.

Reflections can also be personal and caught by the reflector in a variety of formats such as written diaries, personalised videos or taped accounts. Here the person is following a process of their own thought patterns and which can be constructed in different styles. For example it could be an account of a stream of consciousness or an evaluation or description promoted by a set of structured headings and questions, or a mixture of both.

A reflective diary is a common requirement for student learning, promoted in teaching and learning programmes for students who work with people. Probably most of us have kept diaries at some time in our lives. Most of us would rely on them for marking a calendar of events or to catch a descriptive account of community and youth sessions. These types of diaries are useful for catching a description of what has happened and are only part of the reflective process. A reflective diary or journal is intended to be used as a means of communication with yourself about thoughts, ideas, interests; or of your experiences and events. Then these reflections need to be revisited so that you then reflect on your reflections, to further enhance analysis of your event and possibly spot patterns of your working abilities or notice new and different approaches. In this way it can be used as a tool for personal growth and an aid for uncovering creative realisations about your style and approaches and assumptions. It is a useful means of making sense of yourself as a practitioner and your work within a staff team or project. It can be used to uncover new untested thinking about experiences of areas of work you may feel under-rehearsed or unsure of, for example in areas of discrimination by you and others.

It can lead to self-knowledge and insight for future practice. It is a means of stepping back and spotting connections that you have not noticed before (Wheeler, 2007, p345). This connects with the process of reflection-in-action and reflection-on-action explored in the previous section.

The first reflective diaries known of were written by women in Japan in the tenth century and were the first known personal accounts involving both facts and fiction of the times. Diaries of women in medieval England were seen as magical mysterious tools and often treated with suspicion and consequently were frequently burnt along with their owners. In the nineteenth century diaries were used as valued literary tools; the diaries were important as they allowed the diary writers to capture their feelings and aid interpretations of their world. This was then adapted in the twentieth century by the pioneers of psychology (for example Jung 1875–1961). Since then workers with people and 'ordinary people' have adopted the 'diary' as their own creative tool for self-expression and reflection (Rainer, 1980). The reflective diary has also permeated most taught 'working-with-people' courses as a reflective tool for students to evidence their progress in their work-based practices.

As outlined previously, diaries can be structured in a variety of ways. For example a five-step plan in which you (1) record, (2) explain, (3) identify, (4) reflect and (5) note down your learning.

Initially you need to record the facts and description of what you did or observed. Step 2 involves writing an explanation of what you were trying to achieve. Step 3 would involve identifying the influencing factors, e.g. the context and circumstances of your actions. Next you build on the initial description and explanations to start to reflect on the action by asking a range of questions, such as: 'Did I achieve what I wanted? Could I have done something differently? If I had what might have happened?' And finally there is a chance to extract learning for reflecting by asking 'What has the action taught me? Will I change my future practice? In what way?' (adapted from *Understanding Connexions Diploma Assessment Handbook*, 2001, p17).

ACTIVITY 6.2

Think of an activity you have undertaken at work in the last few weeks that went very well. For each question below, write a few notes on reflection of your work.

- *What happened?*
- *What did you do well?*
- *Why did you do it?*
- *What was the outcome for you, for the individual or for the group?*
- *What was it that you did well, they did well and that you could do again?*
- *In what ways could you do it even better next time?*
- *Any further actions you need to take.*

You may find that in doing this on a regular basis you notice more of your effective practice and uncover a whole range of skills and abilities in others and yourself that can build on your professional expertise.

Supervision

The model of supervision will now be explored as a means of reflecting on action and as a process that takes reflections into more depth by engaging within a structured one-to-one or group context.

In particular this section will explore the model of solution-focused (SF) supervision as a means of reflecting-on-action. Solution-focused is an approach that moves away from a problem frame of reference to a problem-free focus, with a directive in finding 'solutions' rather than 'causes'. 'SFBT' (solution-focused brief therapy) is not interested in the causality or nature of problems, but is concerned with seeking solutions to difficulties (Myers, 2008, p21).

Supervision or other forms of learning or mentoring are one of the main methods of reflecting to improve and understand practitioners' work-based practices. The other interactive reflective model accounted for here is the process of developing an enquiry through supervision and supervision models.

Supervision is a common reflective agent where another identified 'supervisor' interacts with the 'supervisee(s)' keeping the focus on the worker, using differing means to prompt, summarise and bounce back the supervisee's interpretations of their work. It could be referred to as an aid for people to learn what they already do as well as a means to uncover and discover new and developing thoughts and interpretations.

Supervision enables the discovery of knowledge and values that underpin practice, discovery of the practitioner's needs and young person's requirements, discovery of good practice and innovative ideas. Essentially 'discovery' is developing thought,

*practice, ideas and interventions – the creation of knowledge that can inform future
practice and policies.*

(Connexions, 2003, p17)

Supervision calls on a range of methods and tools for revealing and exploring the
supervisee's expertise drawn from theoretical approaches including Schön's and Kolb's
thinking. Reflection records are crucial in this process for the supervisee and form the basis
of the evidence for the dialogue between supervisor and supervisee. Often supervision and
supervision approaches have focused on problem-centred models. For example supervisees
are often encouraged or expected to bring to the supervision agenda areas where they feel
they could have done better or are stuck for solutions. Models to deal with this in supervision
have adapted the counselling style of approaches bordering on psychological interpretations
whereby the supervisor delves into past behaviours of the supervisee and explores where
they went wrong and how then to fix it. This approach can encourage the supervisor to be
the expert in the interaction and can by default either disempower or build dependency of
the supervisee on the supervisor. This can reinforce a supervisee's feelings of inadequacy and
can lead to a self-fulfilling expectation of work becoming a problem that then generates the
worker to look for solutions outside their own experiences and of encouraging others to
provide the solution. This is something Thomas (2000) called the guru practice, which can
boost the supervisor's feeling of helping and expertise but can take away the supervisee's
own confidence and ability to build on their skills of uncovering their own solutions to issues.
The SF approach has more recently provided an alternative thinking model whereby the
starting point is that the supervisee has the ability to, and already does, generate ideas for
solutions to their own issues. This is useful for community and youth practitioners as it is
aligned with the understanding of our work-based principle that young people and adult
community members also have the wherewithal to solve their own issues and our job is to
empower them in that process. The next section highlights this approach in reflective
supervision and expands on the tools used in making this happen.

Solution-focused appreciative enquiry model

Appreciative enquiry is a strength based supervision model using solution-focused practice
approaches and methods within a supervision framework. It is a model using the power of
positive framed questions and approaches to create reflective thinking and action of both
supervisee and their work practices. It encourages the reflector to look for any improvements
in their achievements since the last supervision session rather than look for more problems.

Solution-focused practice, sometimes called solution-focused brief therapy (SFBT), was
developed in 1982 in Milwaukee by Steve de Shazer, Insoo Kim Berg and colleagues in North
America who had been working as psychotherapists with indigenous American communities.
They devised a practice of intervention that proved successful and was underpinned by the
following set of empowering beliefs and principles that:

- when people set the goals, changes are more likely to last;
- rapid change is possible when people come up with their own ideas that work;
- small changes can make a big difference – a change in one part of a system can lead to
  changes elsewhere (turning a vicious cycle into a virtuous cycle);

- work is focused on working with the person (or supervisee) rather than the problem;

- look for resources rather than deficits;

- explore possible and preferred futures;

- explore what is currently working;

- treat reflector (or supervisee) as the expert in their own lives.

(adapted from Sharry, 2001, p21)

This focus on solutions is an approach that therefore opposes the traditional problem 'solving' model. This SF model relies on the reflector or supervisee to be the one who comes up with the ideas and solutions and the supervisor's job is therefore to ask the interesting and thought-provoking questions and make observation of workers on their practice.

Solution-focused work, if underpinned by the above set of beliefs and principles, acts as an empowering process. The SF process helps to identify a set of aims, provides a focus on change, helps explore clear goals and preferred futures and builds on strengths, skills and resources. Over the years practitioners have developed and carved out an aligned set of appropriate tools and approaches that can be used to promote this form of positive enquiry (Myers, 2008).

Tools, techniques and questions

Solution-focused tools as described in Wheeler's (2007) account of SF supervision are key to solution-focused work. They include the following key approaches/tools adapted for one-to-one work:

- compliments;

- clarifying goals-scaling, miracle questioning;

- problem-free talk and reframing;

- exceptions;

- reframing and constructive questioning.

(Wheeler, 2007, p347)

The key to the tools are the construction of the supervisors' questions so that the reflector's thinking is directed to problem-free solutions and ideas. The following section describes the key tools used in SF practice.

Compliments

The use of compliments can support and identify skills and strengths of the supervisee (or each member if conducting group supervisions). It could be a useful starter or ice-breaker at the start of a supervisee's journey. As a supervisor in a one-to-one or in a group, you could train yourself to notice things that are useful about people and encourage others to do the same. This provides a positive context in which to undertake the reflective process.

ACTIVITY 6.3

Make a list of 20 things you have done in the last two months.

Of those 20 things, separate those you feel have been useful and successful to you and others, and those you feel were unsuccessful or with which you were dissatisfied. Notice how many items are in the success list in relation to the unsuccessful list.

Make a commitment to share tomorrow at least three things others have done to contribute to your success. Reflect whether this makes a difference in any way.

What you are likely to find is that the items and issues that you feel unsatisfied with are the ones that you recall easily and you therefore create a longer list than of the items that were successful. What people find is that sharing successes focuses our memory on what works and encourages others to do the same. This generates a positive environment to share working practice.

Another way to generate compliments and positive talk would be to ask the supervisee what's working in their current practice and prompt them to expand their list by keeping asking 'what else?' after each contribution. Sometimes the best examples are the ones they contribute nearer the end of this process as they have been well hidden underneath the negative memories.

Clarify goals

Goal clarification supports a positive focus for the supervision conversations and aids clarity, motivation and expectations. For example, useful questions to help ownership of goals include: 'What are you hoping would happen within these supervision sessions?'; 'How will we know we have met them?'; 'What would a good outcome look like?'

Goal setting can also be enhanced with the use of other tools such as the miracle question, exceptions and scaling tools as they help break down goals and identify progress. In other words they help move from vague to clear goals. This builds a clear, detailed and motivating picture of group goals and supports goal setting as a process for change.

Scaling questions

Scaling questions help clarify and evaluate subjective progress. For example the following is an example of using scaling questions for clarifying goal aims (in this case) of the reader's understanding of SF supervision. For example, on a scale 0 to 10 (with 10 being the best understanding you have ever had of SF supervision and 0 being the worst it could ever be) how do you rate yourself right now? The reader could then say '5'. The supervisor would then say 'Great' or 'Okay' and ask: 'Why a 5 and not a 4?' And then 'How could you make it a 6?' and 'How will you know you are at 10?'

From there it's possible for the supervisee to begin to evaluate their progress at each and future sessions by then asking check-scale questions, i.e. 'Things were at 5 last week, so where is it now and why? What would make it one mark higher?' and so on.

The following activity will help to further your understanding of scales and help you practice using this tool.

ACTIVITY 6.4

Think about a hobby/interest that you have. Ask yourself, on a scale of 0–10 (where 0 = you know virtually nothing and 10 = you are the world expert) what number you are on. Let's imagine your answer is 5. Now answer the following questions.

- *What tells you that you are at a 5 and not 0?*
- *What is the highest number you would want to get to?*
- *What would need to happen for you to be 1 point higher up the scale.*

It's also possible that a person feeling very negative about themselves could score a minus number, say -10 or 0. Then as the supervisor you can respond to this in the usual manner by acknowledging this score and say: 'Why that score and not -12?' This scaling question is not a comparative evaluative score system (only in that it can be used in relation to that one person), as one person's 5 could be another person's 7. It is a question that is aimed to explore the factors behind the person's own identified number and then identify the steps it could take for the score to become one or more points higher.

Miracle question

The miracle question supports the uncovering of a future yet to be created. It can encourage motivation to bring about change. It requires the participant or supervisee to first identify a major issue they are facing at the moment that they can't see a way through. Once they have identified this then it is possible for them to explore and create a new future where the problem no longer exists.

ACTIVITY 6.5

Imagine you go to bed and sleep the whole night through. When you wake up, the problem that has been troubling you has been resolved. Look around you.

- *What will be the first small sign that a miracle has happened?*
- *What else will you notice?*
- *What will other people notice about you?*
- *What would you first notice about your surroundings; about yourself and how you feel and act; about others and how they react to you and each other?*
- *What will other people notice about you and others?*
- *What would your day look like; what would you do?*

Using the miracle question encourages new and different information, images and possibly alternative ways to deal with problems or aspirations if they seem far away from the supervisee's starting point. It is an empowering tool that can conjure up in the supervisee often unexpected and creative images and futures from which smaller scaled goals can then be extracted.

Exceptions

Looking for exceptions to practice or events that are a supervisee's concern provides micro solutions to problems or barriers to what is perceived as stuck behaviour or positions and can be very effective, and can provide avenues for future changed approaches.

Exception questions are an exploration of what is happening when the problem isn't around, for example 'when was the last time you were faced with a problem like this and managed to find a way forward?' Close examination of the responses gives clues and hints for future solutions.

It seems to be true that what we instantly recall is every time something hasn't been working. For example, there could be occasions that you find you lose your temper with this one person who is, say, chair of your management committee and a service user of your agency who comes in and points their finger at you and criticises your work. All you can recall is your loss of control of your own response (either angry or submissive) when they appear and start shaking their finger at you and raising their voice, accusing you of doing nothing all day. However, with prompting to answer the exception question 'When was there/recall a time when you didn't lose your temper or didn't feel inadequate in conversation with your chairperson?', the supervisee might then identify a time when the chairperson walked in and didn't wave a finger and been pleasant to you and others. On that day you exchanged pleasantries with them and actually sought them out later on to share and ask for advice on a piece of information about the agency. You were calm and thoughtful and found their advice useful. You realise that that day you had been in an hour beforehand, and had time to do daily tasks and think proactively about areas of the work that would be useful and relevant to share with them.

Being well prepared and calm are characteristics you could now create next time when you are likely to see them again. Here now is an activity for you to explore your 'exceptions'.

ACTIVITY **6.6**

Think of a situation when you were faced with a problem that felt overwhelming. Now start to think about a time when you had faced an apparently overwhelming situation previously and had come through it.

- *What did you do that made a difference?*

- *What would your partner/colleague/friend say they had noticed you doing?*

- *What can you identify about yourself that enabled you to do this?*

For those who are less optimistic about change the exceptions question can be used to identify their own coping strengths by asking 'How do you cope?' or 'What's keeping you going?' This extracts a positive framework to position their current experience and then allows for them to build on their 'coping' exceptions and skills.

Reframing/constructive questions

Questions are 'framed' in such a way that they can produce negative or positive responses. Closed questions achieve information and are often rarely more than one word answers. Together within a negative framework they produce negative responses. However, there is an alternative possibility to reframe the question so it can produce a more open and creative positive response. For example a question negatively framed such as 'How long have you been depressed?' could be reframed to ask 'What would it be like if you weren't depressed?' The latter question would produce a different positive potential reply leading to a further conversation about possibilities of change. Reframing and constructive questioning aims to introduce change, co-operation and collaboration. The SF approach strives to achieve harmony and balanced dynamics through focusing on problem-free talk.

Constructive questions are not used to gather information but generate experiences and new ideas. They focus on strengths and resources and provide positive dynamics that benefit everyone and support goals and problem-free talk. This provides and develops bonds and motivation for change. Solution-free or negative talk creates despair and no hope, and can provide information to aid the identification of the issue but alone it can't create change. Together with solution-focused approach it can construct an appropriate positive approach.

ACTIVITY **6.7**

Here is a good illustration comparing and contrasting traditionally asked problem-focused questions and solution-focused questions (taken from Myers, 2008, p29). The first list gives a number of problem-centred questions that can lead to blame, where the investigating supervisor can become the expert in problem solving, create interpretative analysis sometimes pathological in nature, and devalue the competencies and experiences of the teller.

Problem-focused questions

- *How can I help?*
- *Could you tell me about the problem?*
- *Is the problem a symptom of something deeper?*
- *Can you tell me more about the problem?*
- *How are we to understand the problem in the light of the past?*
- *How many sessions will be needed?*

Think how you could turn these questions around. You may then come up with questions not focused back onto the supervisor's need to solve the issue and find ways to empower the teller in finding their own solutions.

There are times also when an individual behaviour needs to be addressed in order that the supervision process can be effective. Certain dynamics between supervisor and supervisee and within groups can be inhibited by individual behaviour and collective behaviour difficulties (adapted from Sharry (2001) and Preston-Shoot (2007)).

Solution-focused and difficult behaviours

We will now explore four distinct exhibited behaviours – rejecting; scapegoating; monopolising; and being silent – and possible uses of solution-focused tools. The job of a good supervisor is to know when to lead and when to sit back. A good supervisor using solution-focused skills needs to make sure their supervisee or mentee spends significant time in solution talk and problem-free talk that encourages them to come up with their own solutions. The supervisor needs to create a high level of co-operation and collaboration with the ensuing dialogue to encourage interactions between everyone.

The four behaviour issues are now identified and a solution-focused approach is explored.

Rejecting attitude

The issue could be that an individual (or group member) states: 'This isn't working and is not for me.' The facilitator could use reframing technique or exception technique to address this dynamic. For example they could reframe the individual's contribution by saying: 'What is it about your commitment that has kept you involved in the work to date?'

The exception approach could be used by asking the question: 'Tell me a time when supervision has worked for you?' They could also explore the coping skills of the member by asking: 'Given you feel this way and have probably felt this way for a while, then tell me how you have you managed with it so far? What skills have you developed?' (Heap, 1985).

Scapegoating behaviour

Scapegoated/victim issues include a situation where an individual blames others or external issues as the cause for everything that goes wrong. A facilitator's solution could include the reframing of the blame and see it as a compliment, a contribution and opportunity to explore the individual's own commitment for the group to achieve its aims. The blaming could be a result of suppressed feelings of guilt/frustration/fear that resulted in projection in a general way onto the 'others' or circumstances. The supervisor could then encourage an open discussion of the supervisee's suppressed feelings. However, provision may be needed to provide the victim or the scapegoated person with more support or mediation outside the official sessions (if required).

Monopolising behaviour

Those who monopolise the supervision or conversations in general can dominate the sessions such that it restricts you as the supervisor or others at work to contribute and participate.

This can lead to a lack of valuable contributions from you or others, thus preventing effective interventions. The facilitator can intervene and acknowledge the person who monopolises and their contributions, and then take the opportunity to explore how they experience their behaviour and find joint solutions such as limiting their time for contributing and encourage them to find ways for others to participate.

Silent behaviour

The lack of any substantial contribution from an individual can be perceived by you or others as them being judgemental and can make the member who is often silent, invisible in their needs and identity. The supervisor or facilitator is best to not address the silence issue directly but find a way to include them positively, i.e. ask them to comment on a relevant issue or current topic so that you can find an incentive for them to open up and become an equal contributor.

ACTIVITY 6.8

Using the problem behaviours and SF tools listed below, try out solutions to identified problem situations. For example, recall an incident with a person and ask yourself the following questions.

- *What happened (what was the problem behaviour?) and what SF tool might you have used?*

- *Think of a time when you handled that behaviour well with that person (or if stuck with another person exhibiting the same behaviour). What worked for you? How could you do more of that?*

- *Now look at the SF tool you have chosen. Did you use this tool? If yes – how can you use it more often? If no – can you now apply the SF tool you have chosen and imagine how that could work?*

- *Can you identify the skills you have to apply this SF tool?*

- *How does it support equality issues for example in terms of the equal relationship and respect between you and the person?*

Problem behaviours. *Here is a list of potential problem behaviours people have. Pick one of them that you may have already come across and found a hard one to work with.*

- *Monopoliser as avoidance tactics or arrogance.*

- *Silent member.*

- *Scapegoated or victim.*

- *Blamer.*

- *Clown – who used humour as defence.*

- *Negative or rejecting behaviour.*

- *Show off.*

- *Argumentative.*

SF tools. *Here is a list of SF tools. Pick one or more of the tools that you could now use as a means of dealing positively with your chosen behaviour.*

- *Reframing.*

- *Constructive talk.*

- *Finding the exception.*

- *Scaling questions.*

- *Miracle question.*

- *Commenting on what's working.*

What you may find is that your current way of handling one of the problem behaviours is working and does not involve SF tools. If that's the case you may want to check if the tool you use is also respectful and leaves your relationship with them working for further exploration and improvement and change for the better. If so then it is also a useful approach to use. If you have applied your thinking to use a SF tool for the first time, you may want to practise it within a training environment with colleagues before using it within a professional context.

The application of SF tools can support your own behaviour in being aligned with empowerment principles and encourage the recipient to become an expert in their own behavioural changes. Maybe knowing the SF context and tools can add to your repertoire and aid you in being more creative in interventions with colleagues.

Appreciative enquiry EARS model

Appreciative enquiry has developed as a model for SF practice of supervision and also uses the SF tools mentioned previously. It is a process that has been devised from SF thinking and practice and works well after the completion of a first general introductory session.

This first supervision session would be concerned with the creation of the contract with the worker or workers and supervisor. It would give the chance to set the working scene and have the supervisee create a context for their work, maybe express their commitment to their practice (here the miracle question could be useful) and outline their working responsibilities and tasks. It could also explore any changes they would want to happen. The scaling questions are invaluable tools to use for this as they create overall and specific goals and expectations for the best practice they could do. SF practitioners then found that often difficulties subsequently occurred in enabling and encouraging the supervisee to reflect at subsequent sessions about what did happen within a positive framework. So this

EARS model was designed to draw out these changes for the better (Turnell and Hopwood, 1994).

The appreciative enquiry EARS model has four stages: Elicit; Amplify; Reflect; and Start over. These four main stages have been developed as a process of enquiry that has proved to amplify success so as to build a culture of appreciation (Turnell and Hopward, 1994).

Using the EARS process provides a framework to help strengthen workers' reflections of their 'working' progress of change in their practice. It mirrors the solution-focused approach within the supervision process so that it is aligned with the supervisee's solution-focused work practice. This parallel experience not only strengthens both the supervisor's and supervisee's positive reflection process but also builds on their solution-focused work-based practice. However, it is a robust approach that can also be used with a supervisee who, as a practitioner, is not using solution focus in their work.

Each stage of EARS has a set of questions and tools that support the delivery of each particular stage.

Elicit

The beginning question is intended to set the scene so that the supervisee/reflector starts the process in a positive framework (something called a purposive question). For example, at the start of the supervision session the supervisor could start by saying: 'Before we talk about things you are worried about, I'd like to spend 10 minutes hearing about a piece of work you feel proud of'; or 'Tell me about a piece of work-based practice you have done in the last couple of weeks that you feel really proud of'; or 'Tell me about a piece of work-based practice where you were stuck but then managed to move forward.'

This is based on two things: an assumption that change is always occurring in people's practice; and the need to have the supervisee know that improvement is going to be the primary focus of the sessions.

In second and subsequent sessions it is possible to begin by saying: 'What's better than last time's account?'

Amplify

This next stage takes the reflector into creative 'preferred futures' of their thinking about their work. It necessitates drawing out the detail of the behaviour they have just outlined in the elicit question or action taken, by asking Who? What? Where? When? How? The supervisor's role here is to begin to draw out the small details within their account that are indicators of changes in the individual's or group's accounts. It can be hard to know what item or aspect to chase from their account and the supervisor will learn to recognise those areas that are useful from practice.

You as the supervisor may need to locate or anchor their account by asking 'Where did it happen and when did it happen?' This gives you the detail to summarise and feedback to them. The supervisor then needs to continue to clarify the supervisee's account by asking more questions. For example, they could ask 'On that day, in that place, you had a good experience . . .', then follow this with another self-focused question of 'How did you make this happen?' Then they could elicit further detailed information by the use of the following question: 'What did you do?' Once they have answered this question, it is important to ask 'What else?' and then ask again, 'What else?' as a means of encouraging them in uncovering their skills and approaches. It is important to keep asking 'What else?' after each answer as some say that if you haven't asked the question three times, then you haven't asked it at all.

Other useful prompts include asking the following.

- How did you get this started? What did you say/ask?
- Where did you get the idea to do this? Did you have to prepare?
- Was it difficult for you to do it differently like this? What was the hardest part/thing to do?
- What would your boss/co-worker say you did that they found helpful?
- Do you think your colleagues noticed you acting differently? What do you think they would say they had noticed?
- How did you know what you were doing was working?

This way of questioning is not the normal way we have been trained to talk about successes and will, as will any new tool, need practising so that it feels a natural way of enquiring.

To end this session you could ask a scaling question such as: 'How successful were you in your chosen piece of work?' (with 0 = least successful and 10 = the most). You can then respond to scales given as discussed earlier, e.g.: 'A 7. That's good. So tell me the three most important things that you did that make it that high a score for you.' This way you have the supervisee reflect on their own achievements.

Reflection

This stage is designed to reinforce the links with the supervisee's past work so that it can enhance their future practice and can ascribe meaning for the practitioner. This takes a form of enquiry that is in a wider context and draws out from an individual incident or task into their general practice. *The reflective dialogue allows all present in the interview, including the therapist, to consider the significance of the changes* (Turnell and Hopwood, 1994, p57).

It is useful here to ask questions such as the following.

- How have you/she/they done that?
- How has that been different from last week?
- How has that made things different for you (them)?
- How was that helpful?
- How long is it since things have gone this well?
- What does that tell you about them?

Scaling questions are useful in the reflection stage especially in engaging the supervisee to address issues of the supervisee's progression and confidence.

Start over

This is the last stage. Here when a theme runs out of energy or a particular question doesn't seem to make sense to you as the supervisor, or the worker strays off the subject, then start over again with the EARS stages and elicit a new set of questions. At the end of the session it is useful to end with giving the supervisee a task (usually a doing or noticing or thinking task) that is meaningful for them. This is not to be used as a 'must do' but more as an aid at the next session for the dialogue about what's changed.

In SF supervision the supervisee sometimes needs to express everything that's not been working before they can uncover any positive experiences.

> *For us, these are times when the solution-focused therapist is most challenged to have an 'ear to hear' the possible positive developments in a seemingly bleak scenario and the patience and commitment to the belief that the client is the expert in solving their own problems.*

(Turnell and Hopwood, 1994, p63)

ACTIVITY *6.9*

You want to encourage a new worker in your team to develop confidence in their work by using EARS. You are their line manager and their supervisor. They walk into your first session feeling vulnerable and agitated. They begin by talking very fast and quickly about their family holiday and how they haven't settled into a routine. They say they don't think anything is going right and feel very inadequate at work and home.

- *What statement could you say at the outset?*

- *What questions could you start with?*

- *How could you ask a scaling question that would support building their confidence?*

You may have come up with a range of 'setting the scene' statements that welcome people to the team and explain that you don't expect them to start any large responsible tasks until later in their work plan. You need to find an easy way of describing SF and EARS and how you will be drawing on what works in their work and encouraging them to do more of it. The temptation could be not to follow the SF model but to either give them examples of where you see they are succeeding or to explore the negative feelings expressed, i.e. why they feel inadequate. An SF approach would be to ask them to identify what they think they are doing well despite their feelings of being new and inadequate. And ask 'What else?' (three times at least!). Then explore in detail how they are doing 'it' well and what it is that they are doing that makes 'it' work so well. These questions are designed to have the reflector find their own answers in their own practice and empower them to do more of what has been uncovered as already working. The miracle question could also be used to create a bigger context for their preferred future and especially useful if the reflector gets stuck in identifying anything that's working.

So we end with the following case study, as a thought-provoking scenario aimed to explore your reflective abilities and some of the questioning tools of SF practice.

Supervision and equality

You are a worker in a youth worker post attached to a local secondary school in Northumberland, a large rural county. You supervise a whole host of youth workers including full-time assistant Jane who works within the school and the local youth club. She has become less and less motivated since you started a year ago and you are not sure why, though she has expressed a desire to work with the potential emerging new 'girls only group' of female members in the youth club attached to the school. You want to tackle her lack of motivation and girls' group work in your next supervision session. She (you have heard) has recently ended her relationship with her seven-year-long female partner though she has never mentioned it to you. You are someone who is not up on lesbian and gay issues as you thought it had never been necessary for you to know. You go and check the school's policy and are not clear if Section 28 is still in existence – you know it was a legislation that prevented the promotion of homosexuality in schools. Your other part timers who work in the youth club have heard female youth members in the club suggest they want a 'girls' night'. You are not sure if it's right for Jane to become involved with this initiative because of her sexuality and the problems you think it could cause.

- *What are the assumptions and judgements of Jane and her work you are already bringing to supervision?*

- *What could you do to prepare yourself regarding the factual information of the project and girls' work?*

- *What questions would bring out Jane's strengths in her work?*

- *What are your assumptions and what are her desires for her future?*

- *How do you know this?*

- *If you were having SF supervision and were asked what are your goals for the project regarding girls' work what would you think you would say?*

- *Can you identify any of her strengths in the work?*

- *What are the power issues for you as supervisor before you start the process? Real and perceived? (Don't forget to explore the project's geographical influences, such as location, management structure, inherent values, etc.)*

- *How could you address the power issues?*

- *Set an agenda for the next session using EARS and anticipate what areas you could explore regarding Jane and working with girls' work.*

Preparation or reflection for action is important here and for any issue you feel ignorant about or not up to date in regard to discriminated communities. Here for your own preparation (i.e. Cowan's reflection for action) you would be wise to access updated information about lesbian issues. A useful start would be accessing the Stonewall website where you would find out that Section 28 (law in 1988) was repealed in 2003 and that it was a law that was driven by fear rather than legally enforced. Also your organisation should have an equal opportunities policy that should include the need to not discriminate because of anyone's race, disability, gender, age or sexuality. It would be discriminatory of you if you decided she couldn't run a girls' work session because of her sexuality and would indicate that you have a professional training need in regard to your support around challenging homophobia and heterosexism in the workplace.

You could start the sessions by doing an initial exploration of her work and achievements and building trust. At this or possible following sessions you could have her identify her strengths by using compliments to aid her in uncovering her strengths. You could explore exceptions if she persists in only identifying her lack of motivation. You could then use the miracle question to highlight her own goals and aspirations for work and the girls' group and the assets she would bring. (Her experiences of being a lesbian are a positive asset though it would be up to her to bring this into the conversation as your role would be to counteract any hostility about her sexuality from other staff or members by dispelling ignorance and homophobic reactions.) You could then ask her to define specific goals using scaling questions.

You could draw on Thompson's PCS model regarding power and discrimination mentioned in the group work chapter. Future session agenda could be devised between you and Jane and you could then draw on the model outlined in EARS. You are likely to then also identify any further training needs of Jane and your staff team (and indirectly yourself) and explore how she could develop the girls' group.

C H A P T E R   R E V I E W

This chapter has explored reflection and its base in theory and how it relates to practice in community and youth work. It has explored reflection-in-action 'thinking on your feet' and reflection-on-action using records and supervision. In particular it has examined the solution-focused supervision approach using appreciative enquiry. The following table is an attempt to summarise the different steps and stages mentioned in this chapter and link the different actions, approaches and theories.

Time line	Practitioner action	Practitioner context	Theory phase
Before event	Prepare.	Pre-reflection based on previous knowledge or similar experiences.	Reflection-for-action.
At event	Think on your feet.	Reflection instant and based in own experience.	Reflection-in-action.
Just after event	Write/talk about it afterwards.	Reflective diaries.	
Further after event	Engage later in reflective structured dialogue.	Supervision re appreciative enquiry and EARS.	Reflection-on-action.

Figure 6.1 Stages in developing the reflective practitioner

FURTHER READING

For further reading on reflection:

Mark Smith's account in *Local education* is useful and Schön's original account in *The reflective practitioner* (1983).

Schön, D (1983) *The reflective practitioner: how professionals think in action*. Aldershot: Ashgate Publishing.

Smith, MK (1994) *Local education: community, conversation, praxis*. Buckingham: Open University Press.

For more on supervision:

Connexions (2003) *The process of supervision: developing the reflective practitioner*. Sheffield: Connexions.

For solution-focused practice read John Wheeler's account (Chapter 15) in Wheeler, J (2007) 'Solution-focused supervision' in Nelson, TS and Thomas, F (eds) *Handbook of solution-focused brief therapy: clinical applications*. New York: The Hawthorn Press.

Turnell, A and Hopwood, L (1994) 'Solution focused brief therapy: an outline for second and subsequent sessions'. *Case Studies in Brief and Family Therapy*. 8 (2), 52–64.

For creative ways of keeping a journal:

Rainer, T (1980) *The new diary: how to use a journal for self-guidance and expanded creativity*. Sydney: Angus and Robertson.

Bibliography

Beck, U (1992) *Risk society: towards a new modernity*. London: Sage.

Becker, H (1963) *Outsiders: studies in the sociology of deviance*. New York: Free Press.

Belbin, RM (1981) *Management teams: why they succeed or fail*. London: Honeymoon.

Belbin, RM (1993) *Team roles at work*. Oxford: Butterworth-Heinemann.

Bell, C and Newby, H (1971) *Community studies*. London: Allen and Unwin.

Bilton, T with Bradbury, L, Stanyer, J and Stephens, P (2002) *Introductory sociology*. Basingstoke: Macmillan.

Boud, D, Keogh, R and Walker, D (eds) (1985) *Reflection: turning experience into learning*. London: Kogan Page.

Bourdieu, P (1983) The forms of capital, in Richardson, J *The handbook of theory and research for the sociology of education*. New York: Greenwood Press.

Bourdieu, P (1984) *Distinction*. London: Routledge & Kegan Paul.

Bourdieu, P (1992) *Language and symbolic power*. Cambridge: Polity Press.

Bruner, EM (2004) The narrative creation of self, in Angus, LE and McLeod, J (eds) *The handbook of narrative and psychotherapy: practice, theory, and research*. London: Sage.

Burns, D, Heywood, F, Taylor, M, Wilde, P and Wilson, M (2004) *Making community participation meaningful; a handbook for development and assessment*. Bristol: Policy Press.

Button, L (1974) *Developmental group work with adolescents*. London: Hodder and Stoughton.

Byrne, D (1989) *Beyond the inner city*. Buckingham: Open University Press.

Calhoun, C, Gerteis, J, Moody, J, Pfaff, S and Indermohan, V (2007) *Contemporary sociological theory*. Malden, MA: Blackwell.

Cohen, M and Mullender, A (2003) *Gender and groupwork*. London: Routledge.

Collins, P Hill (2000) *Black feminist thought: knowledge, consciousness, and the politics of empowerment*. 2nd edition. New York: Routledge.

Connexions (2001) *Understanding Connexions Diploma Assessment Handbook*. Sheffield: Connexions.

Connexions (2002) *A guide to assessment and the action learning set assessment handbook*. Sheffield: Connexions.

Connexions (2003) *The process of supervision: developing the reflective practitioner*. Sheffield: Connexions.

Cowan, J (2000) *On becoming an innovative university teacher: reflections in action*. Buckingham: Open University Press.

Crossley, N (2005) *Key concepts in critical social theory*. London: Sage.

Crow, G and Allan, G (1994) *Community life: an introduction to local social relations*. Hemel Hempstead: Harvester Wheatsheaf.

DeFilippis, J (2001) The myth of social capital in community development, *Housing Policy Debate*, vol 12: 781–806.

DeFilippis, J (2007) Erasing the community in order to save it? Reconstructing community and property in community development, in Beider, H (ed) *Neighbourhood renewal and housing market: community engagement in the US and UK*. Oxford: Blackwell.

DeFilippis, J and Saegert, S (eds) (2007) *The community development reader*. New York: Routledge.

Department of Communities and Local Government (2008) White Paper *Communities in control: real people, real power*. London: The Stationery Office.

Denzin, N (1989) *Interpretive biography* (Qualitative Research Methods Series No 17.) London: Sage.

Dewey, J (1933) *How we think: a restatement of the relation of reflective thinking to the educative process*. Boston: Heath.

Douglas, T (1978, 2000) *Basic groupwork*. London: Tavistock.

Douglas, T (1993) *Theory of groupwork practice*, London: Macmillan.

Everitt, A and Hardiker, P (1996) *Evaluating for good practice*, Basingstoke: Macmillan.

Foucault, M (1979) *Discipline and punish*. New York: Vintage Books.

Foucault, M (1988) *Politics, philosophy, culture: interviews and other writings 1977–1984*. London: Routledge.

Freire, P (1972) *The pedagogy of the oppressed*. Harmondsworth: Penguin.

Freire, P (1974) *Education: the practice of freedom*. London: Writers and Readers Publishing Cooperative.

Gans, HJ (1962) *The urban villagers*. New York: Free Press.

Garfinkle, H (1967) *Studies in ethnomethodology*. Englewood Cliffs, NJ: Prentice Hall.

George, E, Iveson, C and Ratner, H (1999) *Problem to solution: brief therapy with individuals and families*. London: Brief Therapy Press.

Gibson, A and Clarke, G (1995) *Project based group work facilitator's manual: young people, youth workers and projects*. London: Jessica Kingsley.

Giddens, A (1967) The concept of 'power' in the writings of Talcott Parsons, in Giddens, A *Studies in social and political theory*. New York: Basic Books.

Giddens, A (1991) *Modernity and self identity: self and society in the late modern age*. Cambridge: Polity Press.

Giddens, A (2006) Sociology 5th Edition. Cambridge: Polity Press.

Gilchrist, A (2004) *The well-connected community: a networking approach to community development*. Bristol: Policy Press.

Goodson, I and Sikes, P (2001) *Life history research in educational settings, learning from lives*. Buckingham: Open University Press.

Gramsci, A (1999) *A Gramsci reader: selected writings 1916–1935* (Forgacs, D, ed). London: Lawrence & Wishart.

Grundy, S (1987) *Curriculum: product or praxis*. Lewis: Falmer.

Habermas, J (1987) *Knowledge and human interests*. Oxford: Polity Press.

Hall, S, Clarke, J, Crichter, C, Jefferson, T and Roberts, B (1978) *Policing the crisis: mugging the state and law and order*. London: Macmillan.

Haralambos, M, Heald, RM and Holborn, M (2004) *Sociology themes and perspectives*. London: Collins.

Harding, S (1991) *Whose science, whose knowledge: thinking from women's lives*. Ithaca, NY: Cornell University Press.

Heap, K (1985) The practice of social work with groups. a systematic approach. (National Institute of Social Services Library No 49.) London: Allen & Unwin.

Hedegaard, M (1988) Situated learning and cognition: theoretical learning of cognition, *Mind, Culture and Activity* 5: 2, 114–126.

Henderson, S, Holland, J, McGrellis, S, Sharpe, S and Thomson, R (2007) *Inventing adulthoods: a biographical approach to youth transitions*. London: Sage.

Hillery, GA (1955) 'Definitions of community: areas of agreement' *Rural Sociology* vol 80: 111–23.

Hoggett, P (1997) *Contested communities*. Bristol: Policy Press.

Jay, A (1980) Nobody's perfect – but a team can be, *Observer Magazine*, 20 April 1980.

Kehily, MJ (ed) 2007 *Understanding youth: perspectives, identities and practices*. London: Sage.

Kellner, D (1995) *Media culture*. London and New York: Routledge.

Kolb, DA (1984) *Experiential learning*. New Jersey: Prentice Hall.

Lave, J and Wenger E (1991) *Situated learning: legitimate peripheral participation*. Cambridge: Cambridge University Press.

Lawler, S (2002) Narrative in social research, in May, T (ed) *Qualitative research in action.* London: Sage.

Ledwith, M (2005) *Community development: a critical approach*. Bristol: The Policy Press.

Ledwith, M (2008) 'What is a group?' in Smith, M, *The encyclopaedia of informal education*. **www.infed.org/groupwork/what_is_a_group.htm**

Lees, L (2004) *The emancipatory city*. London: Sage.

Levitas, R (2000) Community, utopia and New Labour. *Local Economy* 15: 188–97

Lewin, K (1952) 'Group decision and social change' in Swanson, GE, Newcomb, TM and Hartley, FE (eds) *Readings in social psychology*. New York: Holt.

Lewin, K, Lippitt, R and White, RK (1939) Patterns of aggressive behaviours in experimentally created social climates. *Journal of Social Psychology*, 10: 271–301

LLUK (2008) The National Occupational Standards for Youth Work. London: Lifelong Learning UK.

Lukes, S (1974) *Power: a radical view*. London: Macmillan.

Macionis, J (2007) *Sociology*. 12th edn. Upper Saddle River, N.J: Pearson/Prentice Hall.

Massey, D (1984) *Spatial divisions of labour*. London: Macmillan.

Mayo, M (1997) *Imagining Tomorrow: community adult education for transformation*. Leicester: NIACE (The National Institute of Adult Continuing Education).

Mehrabian, A (1971) *Silent messages: implicit comunication of emotions and attitudes*. Belmont, CA: Wadsworth.

Mies, M (1993) Towards a methodology for feminist research, in Hammersley, M (ed) *Social research, philosophy, politics and practice*. London: Sage.

Mintzberg, H (2005) Developing theory about the development of theory, in Smith, KG and Hitt, MA (2005) *Great minds in management*. Oxford: Oxford University Press.

Mirza, H Safia (2008) *Race, gender and educational desire*. London: Institute of Education, University of London.

Mullender, A and Ward, D (1991) *Self-directed groupwork: users take action for empowerment*. London: Whiting and Birch.

Myers, S (2008) *Solution-focused approaches*. Lyme Regis: Russell House Publishing.

Nelson, TS and Thomas, F (eds) (2007) *Handbook of solution-focused brief therapy: clinical applications*. New York: The Hawthorn Press.

Oakley, A (2005) *The Ann Oakley reader: gender, women and social science*. Bristol: Policy Press.

Oko, J (2008) *Understanding and using theory in social work*. Exeter: Learning Matters.

O'Leary, Z (2004) *The essential guide to doing research*. London: Sage.

Packham, C (2008) *Active citizenship and community learning*. Exeter: Learning Matters.

Pahl, RE (1966) The rural urban continuum. *Sociolgia Ruralis*, 6: 229–329, reprinted in Pahl, RE (1968) *Readings in urban sociology*. London: Pergamon Press.

Parekh, B (2008) *A new politics of identity: political principles for an interdependent world*. Basingstoke: Palgrave Macmillan.

PLAN UK Summary Report (2009) Because I am a girl: the state of the world's girls. London: PLAN.

Preston-Shoot, M (2007) *Effective groupwork*. Basingstoke: Palgrave Macmillan.

Putnam, RD (2000) *Bowling alone: the collapse and revival of American community*. New York: Simon and Schuster.

Rainer, T (1980) *The new diary: how to use a journal for self-guidance and expanded creativity*. Sydney: Angus and Robertson.

Rex, J and Moore, R (1967) *Race, community and conflict: a study of Sparkbrook*. Oxford: Oxford University Press.

Robson, C (1993) *Real world of research: a resource for social scientists and practitioner-researchers*. Oxford: Blackwell.

Scott, CD and Jaffe, DT (1991) *Empowerment: building a committed workforce*. London: Kogan Page.

Scott, J (2006) *Social theory: central issues in sociology*. London: Sage.

Schön, D (1983) *The reflective practitioner: how professionals think in action*. Aldershot: Ashgate Publishing.

Schostak, J (2006) *Interviewing and representation in qualitative research*. Buckingham: Open University Press.

Sharry, J (2001) *Solution-focused group work*. (Brief Therapy Series). London: Sage.

Smart, S (2007) Informal education, (in)formal control? What is voluntary youth work to make of self-assessment? *Youth and Policy*, 95: 73–82.

Smith, KG and Hitt, MA (2005) *Great minds in management*. Oxford: Oxford University Press.

Smith, MK (1994) *Local education: community, conversation, praxis*. Buckingham: Open University Press.

Smith, MK (2001, 2006) Evaluation, in *The encyclopaedia of informal education*. **www.infed.org/biblio/b-eval.htm**

Smith, MK (2008) What is a group? in *The encyclopaedia of informal education*. **www.infed.org/groupwork/what_is_a_group.htm**

Spence, J (2009) In defence of intellectually rigorous youth work. **http://indefenceofyouthwork.wordpress.com/2009/08/19/in-defence-of-intellectually-rigorous-youth-work/**

Spender, D (1980) *Man made language*. London: Routledge & Kegan Paul.

Stacey, M (1969) The myth of community studies. *British Journal of Sociology*, 20 (2): 134–47.

Stonewall website: **www.stonewall.org.uk**

Thomas, FN (2000) Mutual admiration: fortifying your competency based supervision experience. *RATKES: Journal of the Finnish Association for the Advancement of Solutions and Resources Orientated Therapy and Methods*, 2: 30–39.

Thompson, J (1988) Adult education and the women's movement, in Lovett, T (ed) *Radical approaches to adult education: a reader*. London: Routledge.

Thompson, J (1997) *Words in edgeways: radical learning for social change*. Leicester: NIACE (The National Institute of Adult Continuing Education).

Thompson, N (1996) *People skills: A guide to effective practice in human services*. London: Macmillan.

Thompson, N (2001) *Anti discriminatory practice*. Basingstoke: Macmillan.

Tuckman, BW (1965) Developmental sequence in small groups. *Psychological Bulletin*, 63: 6, 384–399. This article was reprinted in *Group Facilitation: A Research and Applications Journal* – Number 3 Spring 2001 and is available as a Word document: **http://dennislearningcenter.osu.edu/references/GROUP%20DEV%20ARTICLE.doc**

Tuckman, BW (1984) Citation classic – Developmental sequence in small groups. *Current Contents Number 34*. Available as a pdf file: **www.garfield.library.upenn.edu/classics1984/A1984TD25600001.pdf**

Turnell, A and Hopwood, L (1994) Solution focused brief therapy: an outline for second and subsequent sessions. *Case Studies in Brief and Family Therapy*, 8 (2): 52–64.

Twelvetrees, A (2008) *Community work*, 4th edition. Basingstoke: Palgrave Macmillan.

Wheeler, J (2007) Solution-focused supervision, in Nelson, TS and Thomas, F (eds) *Handbook of solution-focused brief therapy: clinical applications*. New York: The Hawthorn Press.

White, M and Epston, D (1990) *Narrative means to therapeutic ends*. London: WW Norton and Co.

Wiessner, C (2005) Storytellers: women crafting new knowing and better worlds. Convergence, XXXVIII (4), 101–119.

Wirth, L (1938) Urbanism as a way of life. *American Journal of Sociology* 44 (1): 1–24.

Worsley, P (1988) *The new introducing sociology*. Harmondsworth: Penguin.

Index